Walking in Newness of Life

Experiencing the Power of God in Resurrection by
Identifying with Christ in His Death and Burial

Beth Hogan

Walking in Newness of Life

Experiencing the Power of God in Resurrection by
Identifying with Christ in His Death and Burial

What shall we say then? Are we to continue in sin that grace may abound? By no means! How can we who died to sin still live in it? Do you not know that all of us who have been baptized into Christ Jesus were baptized into his death? We were buried therefore with him by baptism into death, in order that, just as Christ was raised from the dead by the glory of the Father, we too might walk in newness of life.

Romans 6:1-4

WALKING IN NEWNESS OF LIFE
© 2014 Beth Hogan
ISBN 978-1-4997-7117-6
Published by Annabeth Publishing
Cover Image Photo Daniel Hogan Today
Printed August 5, 2014

To Dan,
Our wedding Psalm says it all.

Psalm 126

When the Lord restored the fortunes of Zion, we were like those who dream. Then our mouth was filled with laughter, and our tongue with shouts of joy; then they said among the nations, "The Lord has done great things for them." The Lord has done great things for us; we are glad.

Restore our fortunes, O Lord, like streams in the Negeb! Those who sow in tears shall reap with shouts of joy! He who goes out weeping, bearing the seed for sowing, shall come home with shouts of joy, bringing his sheaves with him.

Always, b.

CONTENTS

Acknowledgments

I would like to acknowledge and thank several people for their prayer support and encouragement as I wrote these devotional essays. I think first of the New York crowd: Deborah Bontrager, Brigid and Michael Callahan, Erin Hill, and Steve and Vanessa Sumnick. You were all used by the Lord to encourage me to step out on faith and keep believing God when the desire to write this book was first forming in my soul. Thank you for your prayers and encouragements!

Also, thank you to Pastor Rob and Beth Elliott. Beth, you have been a true friend and a great encouragement to me in the Lord. Thank you for encouraging me to trust the Lord, thank you for your faithful prayer support, and thank you for being such a great example of Christlikeness. I love you in the Lord!

Thank you especially to those in the Greentown Bible Fellowship Church family who prayed for this writing. Pastor Johnston and Lori, thank you for loving me and my family in the Lord. Pastor, thank you for your faithful shepherding care of our family, for encouraging me to write this book, and your very helpful feedback after reading the first draft. Lori, thank you for loving me in the Lord, thank you for your tender words of admonition and encouragement, and for setting such a godly example for me to follow.

Also, thank you to LeeAnn LoMonaco for inviting me to the prison-without which I would not have taken the time to write this book. Thank you, also, to Miss. Carly Smith and Miss. Kelly Smith for your faithful prayers, you are both a sweet blessing to me in the Lord. Thank you also to Mrs. Louise Hill, you will never know (until glory, I suppose) how much your prayers and weekly encouragement mean to me. Thank you also to Ed and Heather McEnaney both of whom prayed for this writing to be accomplished. Especially, thank you to Heather, who repeatedly asked me how the writing was progressing and encouraged me to keep going when I wanted to give up. A hardy thank you to Mollie and Jason Kleber who prayed with me as this work was being revised and completed. Mollie, I am so glad the Lord brought you to your old home town (for a season), and while you were here, you were willing to make some new friends! And, of course, a great thank you to Jackie and Simon Manning. Jackie, I really believe that without your faithful prayers and constant encouragements I would not have completed this undertaking. Thank you so much, you are a true sister and friend in the Lord!

I also want to thank my five blessed children; Abby, Becky, Sam, John, and Elijah. You are the best kids in the whole world! Your father and I consider you our joy and crown (1 Thessalonians 2:19-20). We love you, and we are so pleased in the Lord with you all! Thank you for praying for me to have the courage, patience, and the wisdom needed for writing, and thank you for giving me up to this task. Thank you, especially, Abby and Becky for all the hard work you both did on my behalf: helping with the cover and in the editing of this book; as well as, making dinners, keeping up with the housework, and sometimes, even, sacrificing our *girl time* together so that I could write.

Finally, thank you to my husband, Dan. Thank you loving me through the good times and the hard times. Thank you for serving me and our children with your love, faithfulness, protection, provision, care, and leadership. Thank you for shepherding me by faithfully washing me with the Word and praying for me. Most of all, thank you for loving Jesus Christ with a steady love; a *"long obedience in the same direction"* sort of love. The Lord has used you, more than anyone else on the face of this earth, to bless me, teach me, encourage me, and grow me up in Him. I am so thankful that He has called us to be co-heirs, walking in newness of life together. Also, thank you for using your skills and eye for detail to help design the cover and publish the final copy of this book. You are my Best Beloved, and I love you. I love you. I love you. Forever. Forever. Forever.

My Red Sea Experience

I was raised in a non-Christian home. However, as a girl I attended Vacation Bible School and Sunday School at a neighborhood church. Eventually, I became very involved with the youth ministry program of this church. Through my involvement in these youth ministries, I professed a desire that (when I died) I would be saved from hell and go to heaven to be with Jesus. As a result of this professed desire, a trusted male youth leader led me in what Christians commonly call "the sinner's prayer" (This is a prayer of confession of one's sins and profession of one's faith in Christ for the forgiveness of sins.) Shortly after this event, the same youth leader began to have one-on-one Bible study and counseling sessions with me, and within months of my profession of faith, he began to abuse me sexually.

After several years of the abuse, I walked away from the Church of Jesus Christ. I then intentionally dove into a pit of sin, rebellion, and self-destruction. Upon graduation from high school, I had very few viable life options to choose from, and as the Sovereign Lord would have it, I enlisted in the United States Army Reserve. I was eighteen years old.

Before leaving for basic training, I was given a pocket New Testament that I carried with me and read throughout the early weeks of my training. One day, I read something that would change me forever. I read, "...God shows his love for us in that while we were still sinners, Christ died for us" (Romans 5:8). As I read that verse, I thought to myself, 'Well, I'm a sinner - that means that Christ died for me.' It was then that I realized that Jesus Christ had died specifically for me. So there I was standing all alone in a training field in Fort Jackson, South Carolina, and I came to saving faith in the Lord Jesus Christ.

After this realization, to the very best of my ability, I lived in obedience to whatever I read in the Bible. I reasoned that since Jesus was my Savior - He was, therefore, my LORD as well. As for the abuse of the past, I figured the right thing to do was just to forgive and forget. So, after basic and technical training, I went home, found a solid Bible believing church, met my husband, got married, and began having a family.

In large measure, I was greatly blessed by God. I had a husband who loved the Lord and honored me with his love, provision, and faithfulness. I had one amazing child after another. All my physical and emotional needs were provided and I even had ample opportunities for serving the Lord in my home church. Still, something was wrong with my life, and it had been wrong all along - I just couldn't put my finger on what it was.

I knew that something was "off" in my soul primarily because of the descriptions of the normal Christian life outlined in Scripture. Statements like the ones that Jesus made in the Gospel of John: "Whoever believes in me, as the Scripture has said, "Out of his heart will flow rivers of living water." and another, "I came that they may have life and have it abundantly" (John 7:38, 10:10). It was from reading verses like these and from a growing awareness of my inability to emotionally connect with the Lord and with other believers that I knew something wasn't as it should be in my relationship with Christ. I was not living the fruitful Christian life that Jesus had promised to give His followers. No doubt, I was blessed by God, but something seemed to be blocking the flow of the living streams in my soul. In short, I was not experiencing the abundant life that Christ had died to give me - and I had no idea why.

As the years passed, I was becoming increasingly frustrated with this situation. I kept praying for and waiting to experience the abundance, joy, peace, and love that the Bible promised. But to me it seemed as though with time I was becoming angrier, more anxious, and growing increasingly depressed. I was trying to do everything that I knew a woman who professed Christ as Lord should be doing. I was daily in the Word and prayer. I was living in submission to God, my husband, and my church leaders. I was raising my children in the fear and admonition of the Lord. I was caring for my home and serving God in the church. Nonetheless, I felt as though I was becoming emotionally numb and I was becoming more and more disappointed by the lack of joy, peace, and abundance in my walk with Christ.

One day in my frustration, I exclaimed, "Lord, You must be angry with me!" With that heart's cry, I felt a startling impression in my soul - the Lord was not angry with me, I was the one that was angry with the Lord. The thought that I was angry with the Lord didn't make any sense at all to me... Why would I be angry with the Lord? But, not long after this the Lord led me to read Psalm 51:6, "Behold, you delight in truth in the inward being, and you teach me wisdom in the secret heart." This verse applied to my situation, but, how?

I began to pray over this verse and ask the LORD how it applied to my life - why I had felt a prompting from the Spirit when I read it. And, in His time, God answered me. In the way that only the Lord can speak to the soul, He began to show me that I was angry because I had never allowed Him to take the venom of the past abuse out of me after I turned towards the Lord in repentance for salvation. The Lord showed me that I had refused to acknowledge that the sexual abuse, which I had endured as a girl, had any effect on me. God began to reveal to me the truth that I had been living in willful denial.

My denial was nothing but self-deceit and God wanted me to allow the truth about the effects of the abuse to be acknowledged. He wanted me to admit that part of me was broken so that I could experience His healing grace. My willful denial had been a cloak that I had been using in an attempt to cover over the anger, disappointment, and hurt, which I felt as a result of the abuse. In short, I needed to acknowledge the truth that I was angry about what had happened in the past; that I was angry about the abuse.

Part of the truth that I needed to acknowledge about the abuse was that I was angry because of my incorrect understanding of God's seeming indifference towards the abuse. The Lord began to show me that I wrongly viewed God as an indifferent Sovereign Bystander and Silent Witness to the abuse. For this reason, instead of going to God with a humble heart, asking Him for understanding and healing I had allowed my denial, rather my own self-deception, to lead me down the dangerous path of infringing on the integrity of God. The truth was I needed to repent of my self-deceit and self-sufficiency; I needed to ask God to forgive me for my sins of pride, presumption, and bitterness. (The sins, which had resulted from not understanding that my Heavenly Father is all-knowing and perfectly wise in bestowing all of life's providences - even the painful ones.) Then, I needed to - *with vulnerable faith* - place my brokenness in His sovereign hands.

As I did this, I felt out of control and overwhelmed with emotions. It would be impossible for me to explain the depths of the sorrow and confusion that I felt at that time in my life. I kept asking myself, 'What can I do with my past?' 'Where can I go with my anger, disappointment, and hurt?' 'Why am I dealing with this now?' 'Will any of this ever make sense?' 'Can any of this ever make sense?' Ultimately, the Lord showed me that it was at the cross of Christ (and only at the cross of Christ) that these questions could be answered. The cross was the only place where my past, my brokenness, and God's sovereignty made any sense at all to me. As I brought my brokenness and messed up past to the cross of Christ, I began to see not just the cross of Christ, but I began to see the Christ of the cross.[1]

---

[1] Dr. D.A. Carson's *How Long O Lord? Reflections on Suffering and Evil* was of great help to me in understanding how God uses the pain in our lives to point us to the cross of Christ. The Lord especially used the third part of his book, "Glimpses of the Whole Puzzle: *Evil and Suffering in the World of a Good and Sovereign God*" to minister to me. I am very thankful for this work. Although, I know of no direct quote or reference from this book in my testimony (or this entire devotional), I would like to acknowledge that several of Dr. Carson's books

By saying 'I began to see the Christ of the cross' I mean that I began to understand (in an emotional and experiential way, not just in an abstract theological way) the magnitude of what Christ did in His incarnation and atoning work on my behalf. I started to grasp the weight of the truth that Jesus, of His own volition, had identified Himself with my frailty through the incarnation, and then had willfully identified Himself with my brokenness on the cross. As a result of this deeper understanding of the Lord's cross-work, I found that Christ was not the indifferent Sovereign Bystander that I had wrongly imagined Him to be. (May the Lord forgive me for my foolish pride and unbelief in thinking this way.) Instead, I found that He was the voluntary Sovereign Substitute, who had identified Himself with my shame through His cross. I found that He was not at all the Silent Witness to those dark deeds of the past but that He was the Silent Lamb, who had been slaughtered for them. I began to experience in real time, as it were, the powerful truth that the Christ bore my grief and carried my sorrow. And, furthermore, I began to understand how it was that '...by His stripes..." I would be healed (Isaiah 53:5).

Understanding that the Lord willfully identified Himself with me in my frailty and sin-induced brokenness through His cross gave me the divinely empowered courage, which I needed, to entrust my own brokenness and hurt to Him. In practical terms, I did this by learning how to identify my sufferings with Him in His cross-suffering. It was through the process of identifying with the Lord in His cross-work that *I was enabled to acknowledge the painful truths about my past* and that I learned to trust God with the death, or brokenness, which had resulted in my life from the abuse. By meditating on the suffering and death that Jesus had endured on

---

(and this one in particular) have directly impacted my understanding of God and His sovereign love for me in the midst of my own pain and suffering.

Carson, D.A. 2006. *How Long O Lord? Reflections on Suffering and Evil* 2nd ed. Grand Rapids, Michigan: Baker Academic.

the cross for me and my sin, I was able to acknowledge the suffering and death that I had endured in the years of abuse. I was enabled to acknowledge the reality that death had occurred in my soul; as a result, of the abuse. By faith, I came to grips with the truth that, until glory, parts of my soul would always be gone or at least altered by what had happened in those years.

In identifying with the Lord Jesus Christ in the burial, *I learned to accept my past.* I learned to trust God with the corpse of my childhood soul, or rather, I learned to trust the Lord with the consequences of having been abused as a child. For me, this was the most trying aspect of the process of healing. It was like, in Jude 1:9 where we read that Michael the Archangel and Satan fought over the body of Moses. I was fighting with the Holy Spirit about the body of that young girl by refusing to acknowledge and accept the depths of my sorrow over the losses that I had incurred in the experience of abuse. I had to bury the thoughts of what could have been, what should have been, the memory of what was, and learn to trust God with my broken, shameful realities. Seeing the truths of the burial of Christ in the Scripture, I learned how to submit to God's ordaining purposes in suffering, how to bury the seed of my past in the borrowed tomb with Christ; in the hope that God would redeem it from the grave in resurrection new life. By faith, I had to entrust myself to the hope of Scripture: "Truly, truly unless a grain of wheat falls into the earth and dies - it remains alone, but if it dies it bears much fruit" (John 12:24).

I did not know it at the time, but consciously identifying with the Lord Jesus Christ in His death and His burial was the beginning of truly experiencing the power of the resurrection of Christ for walking in newness of life. As I fellowshipped with the Man of Sorrows through my own afflictions, and learned to fellowship with Him in His burial; God began to resurrect the parts of my soul that had died in the past abuse by transforming me in the present. It was at this time in my life that I began to experience the powerful reality of the doctrine of my union with Christ. By learning to identify with Christ in His cross-death, burial, and resurrection life, the curses of my past increasingly became the blessings of my present.

In all of this, I came to understand in a very personal way the massive and life-changing reality of the sovereign power and deep love of God. The awesome truth that God is most certainly and most emphatically sovereign over all things in life - working them all to the end for my good and His glory- became an experiential reality for me. For, the Lord began to show me that the abuse that I had endured was my own personal Red Sea experience - a life changing providence which led me to a desperate need of experiencing the awesome power of God in resurrection. The abuse was just one example of God's perfect ordering of my life. It was just one of the many sovereign graces of my life that the Lord had ordained to the end that I would turn to Christ in saving faith; experience the powerful redemption of the cross, and know the depth of the love of God more intimately through my union with Christ.

At this time in my Christian life, I began to view each of my life experiences - from the afflictions to the blessings and all the little events in between, as opportunities to identify with Christ in His death, burial, and resurrection-power for walking in newness of life. In short, I began to live my life in the conscious awareness that "...all of us who have been baptized into Christ Jesus were baptized into his death. We were buried, therefore, with him by baptism into death, in order that, just as Christ was raised from the dead by the glory of the Father, we too might walk in newness of life" (Romans 6:3-4).

A Word to the Reader

The following is an account of the truths that God used to resurrect the parts of my soul that had died as a result of the sins that were committed against me in the experience of having been sexually abused. When I say that God used the following truths to resurrect the parts of my soul that had died in the abuse, I simply mean that He has used the following applications of His Word to heal my sin-induced brokenness. The applications that I have presented in this devotional are really just my (best effort) attempt to share how God has applied His Word to my life and my particular circumstances. Even so, the truths themselves are universal truths that the Lord uses in the lives of all believers to cause them to grow in holiness.

While the essays do not have to be read in any particular order, I have ordered them, in a way, which (I think) will be most helpful to the reader. *Part One: The Sanctified* consists of essays that review the basic and fundamental teachings of Christianity. The essays of week one consist of understanding the essential foundational teachings of the Christian faith. The essays of the second week are geared toward understanding some of the more advanced Christian doctrines. *Part Two: The Sanctifying Cross* consists of the essays that review the process of sanctification (becoming holy) in its relationship to the Lord's call to the cross. Week three primarily consist of understanding the practical ways that a believer can answer the call to the cross for the sake of her sanctification. Finally, the essays of the fourth week all center on appropriating (laying hold of or making one's own) the resurrection power of God in the cross of Christ by identifying with Him in His death and burial. I strongly recommend that the reader work through this collection of devotions in the order that they are presented. You will find that I have defined relevant terms in the first two weeks of essays that are necessary for understanding the concepts presented in the final two weeks of this book.

Also, it is best to let the content of each essay "sit" for a day or so before moving on to the next one. This advice is especially helpful in reading the second half of the book, as the essays of the third week begin to focus specifically on the aspect of emotional healing in the process of sanctification. Thus, it is those essays that may become somewhat heavy reading for women who have experienced any form of emotionally traumatizing sin.

By emotionally traumatizing sin, I mean those sins that are of a particularly disturbing nature; such as, having had an abortion, having been subjected to physical, sexual, or prolonged emotional abuse, or (perhaps even worse) living with the knowledge that someone you love was physically, sexually, or emotionally abused. Other examples of sins that are traumatizing would include experiencing the unfaithfulness of a spouse through the act of adultery, or experiencing other betrayals of relational trust such as divorce, neglect, and, abandonment. These sorts of sins always result in some form of death or emotional brokenness in the human soul, as all sin does (James 1:15). And, the magnitude of the negative emotional effects of experiencing these types of sins cannot be overstated. I have shared truths in this 28 day devotional that the Lord has graciously taken nearly twenty years to begin to work out in my life; truths that He will probably continue to work out in me until glory. It is for this reason that I encourage the reader not to rush through the devotions of the last two weeks. Instead, a prayerful consideration of their contents will help the reader from being overcome with emotion by the truths that they contain.

My desire is that those who read this devotional will be set free from their sin, their past, their shame, and their brokenness - as I have been set free from mine. My hope for this book is twofold. First, it is that each one reading will experience the power of God through her union with Christ in His death, burial, and resurrection. My second hope is that each one who reads these pages will come to a personal experiential understanding of the sovereign power and deep love of God, as they see how He works all the events of our lives out for the good of His people and the glory of His grace.

With that said, I have specifically written this devotional for the women in the Pike County Corrections Facility H.O.P.E Program. I have written this for you because I know (from personal experience) that true freedom is only ever experienced through the resurrection power of God that is extended to us through the living Lord Jesus Christ. By the soul-resurrecting power of God, extended to me in Christ, I have been set free from everything that was killing me: my past, my pain, my addictions, my sin, and my brokenness. By God's grace, I now live in the joyful freedom of walking in newness of life in Christ. It is now and will continue to be my prayer that this book might be of some help to you to the same end: that by God's merciful grace you also will be set free from everything that is killing you: your past, your pain, your addictions, your brokenness, and your sin; so that by God's grace you also will be truly free - to joyfully walk in newness of life in Christ.

Beth Hogan
Milford, Pennsylvania
July 29, 2014.

Part 1: The Sanctified

Then Moses said to Aaron, "This is what the LORD has said: 'Among those who are near me I will be sanctified, and before all the people I will be glorified.'"　　　　　　　　　*Leviticus 10:3*

And such were some of you. But you were washed, you were sanctified, you were justified in the name of the Lord Jesus Christ and by the Spirit of our God.　　　　　　　　　*1 Corinthians 6:11*

And now I commend you to God and to the word of his grace, which is able to build you up and to give you the inheritance among all those who are sanctified.　　　　　　　　　*Acts 20:32*

Sanctify them in the truth; your word is truth.　　　　　　　　　*John 17:17*

Thus saith the Lord GOD; I do not this for your sakes, O house of Israel, but for mine holy name's sake, which ye have profaned among the heathen, whither ye went. And I will sanctify my great name, which was profaned among the heathen, which ye have profaned in the midst of them; and the heathen shall know that I am the LORD, saith the Lord GOD, when I shall be sanctified in you before their eyes. For I will take you from among the heathen, and gather you out of all countries, and will bring you into your own land. Then will I sprinkle clean water upon you, and ye shall be clean: from all your filthiness, and from all your idols, will I cleanse you. A new heart also will I give you, and a new spirit will I put within you: and I will take away the stony heart out of your flesh, and I will give you an heart of flesh. And I will put my spirit within you, and cause you to walk in my statutes, and ye shall keep my judgments, and do them. And ye shall dwell in the land that I gave to your fathers; and ye shall be my people, and I will be your God."　　　　　　　　　*Ezekiel 36:22-29, KJV*

Day 1: Thinking about God

Holy, holy, holy, is the Lord God Almighty,
who was and is and is to come! Revelation 4:8

The first step that anyone takes in walking in newness of life is the step of learning how to think about God in a right way. To think about God in a right way, we must first understand that *God is holy.* In saying that God is holy, we mean that God is *set-apart, distinct, different, and other in every way.* God is distinct, different, and other, from everything and everyone else that now exists, that ever has existed, or that ever will exist. In other words, God is set apart unto Himself; He is in a class of His own. For example, God is set apart unto Himself in that He is self-existent. This means that God exists and sustains His existence by His own power. God is truly the only Autonomous Being who has ever or will ever exist. Contrary to the thinking of many people, God did not evolve, appear, develop, or find His birthplace in the heart's imagination of man. Neither is God a force, or a vague mystical power. He is the Eternal Spirit who never had a beginning and whom will never end (Job 36:26; Isaiah 46:8-11; John 4:24). God is a real Personal Being that has always and will always self-exist.

God is also holy in that He has a divine nature (2 Peter 1:4). Saying that God has a divine nature means that the essence of who God is, the features and the qualities that make God who He is, are divine and beyond human understanding (Isaiah 40:28; Romans 11:33). For, God thinks divine thoughts; He thinks in a way that only God thinks (Isaiah 55:8; Romans 11:33-36). God feels divine feelings; that is, God feels in a way that only God can feel (Genesis 6:6; Mark 3:5; Ephesians 4:30). And, God wills (determines, intends) divine plans; God wills and purposes in a way that only God can choose and plan (Ephesians 1:5-9, 3:1-11). In all of this, God thinks, feels, and wills with perfect understanding, perfect knowledge, and absolute purity. Every trait of God is both perfect and unchanging in its perfection. For, God is God and no-one else is God. God alone is perfectly holy in His divine nature; therefore, God is the only being who is set apart from all others in every way. That is why, God says about Himself, "I am God, and there is no other; I am God, and there is none like me…" (Isaiah 46:9).

When we say that God is holy we also mean that God is *perfectly morally pure, sinless, upright, and containing nothing exceptionable.* Therefore, God has never sinned in thought, word, or deed. God never does anything wrong, nor is He ever the author of any evil temptation. The Bible says, "…God cannot be tempted by evil, nor does he tempt anyone…" (James 1:13b, NIV). God is morally perfect - He always has been, and He always will be. He is clean, pure, sinless, upright, righteous, good, kind, long-suffering, patient, merciful, full of grace, compassionate, peaceful, sincere, truthful, and in every other possible way: God is morally perfect. For, God is never dishonest. He never lies, cheats, or sneaks. He is never unfaithful, never un-wise, never unwilling or incapable of doing what is right. And, since God is unchanging; He will never not be perfectly morally upright. That is why the Bible says, "The Rock, his work is perfect, for all his ways are justice. A God of faithfulness and without iniquity, just and upright is He." And, in another place the Word says, "Jesus Christ is the same yesterday and today and forever" (Deuteronomy 32:4; Hebrews 13:8).

One of the main ways that God is set-apart unto Himself (holy) is that God alone is *sovereign* (Ezekiel 12:28; Acts 2:24; Revelation 6:10). To be sovereign is to be *unrestricted in power and absolute domination, confessing no limitations or restraints.* In layman's terms this means that God is in control, totally and completely in control of everything, everywhere, all the time. As the Bible says, "…He does according to his will among the hosts of heaven and among the inhabitants of the earth, and none can stay his hand or say to him, "What have you done?" (Daniel 4:35). Unlike all created entities (angels, humans, animals, everything but God), God is not dependent upon any outside source for anything at all. God never has to ask permission. God never needs help, aid, counsel, approval, or affirmation: He does what He wants to do, when He wants to do it, how He wants to do it, and He does it despite how people may feel about it. Only God is sovereign; because only God has absolute and unrestricted, unlimited power and domination. For this reason, King David prayed, "Yours, O LORD, is the greatness and the power and the glory and the victory and the majesty, for all that is in the heavens and in the earth is yours. Yours is the kingdom, O LORD, and you are exalted as head above all… In your hand are power and might, and in your hand it is to make great and to give strength to all" (1 Chronicles 29:11-12).

Since God is holy in every way possible; God is glorious in the most possible way. To say that God is glorious means that God is worthy of fame and admiration; that God has striking beauty and splendor that evokes feelings of delighted admiration in us. *God's glory is the overflowing radiance and the brilliance of the holiness of God (i.e., the set-apart-ness of God) which calls forth our worship, admiration, and praise.* God's glory is the revelation of the surpassing magnificence, beauty, and value of Who God is in all of His perfect characteristics. His perfect love, His sovereignty, His patience, His kindness, His wisdom, His loveliness, and all of His other perfections make God desirable, delightful, pleasing, admirable, and glorious. One Bible teacher explains God's glory like this, "The glory of God is the holiness of God put on display. That is, it is the infinite worth of God made manifest."[2] This is why in God's throne room, the great

---

[2] Piper, John. 2011. *Rebuilding Some Basics of Bethlehem: The Centrality of the Glory of God.* http://www.desiringgod.org/articles/rebuilding-some-basics-of-bethlehem-the-centrality-of-the-glory-of-god. July 31, 2014.

Piper, John. 2012. *Soli Deo Gloria.* http://www.ligonier.org/learn/articles/soli-deo-gloria/. April 19, 2014.

seraphim cry out, "Holy, holy, holy is the Lord of hosts; the whole earth is full of his glory!"(Isaiah 6:3).

God created everything that exists in order to manifest (or to make known) His glory. All matter was created to give us a small glimpse, a physical picture, of the incomprehensible greatness of who God is. Do you think that fruit is sweet? God is sweeter than the sweetest of fruit. Do you think that the sun is dazzlingly brilliant? God is dazzlingly brighter still. Do you think cool water is refreshing on a hot summer's day? God is more refreshing than a thousand thirst-quenching mountain springs. Do you think that the ocean is vast? The vastness of God is greater still. Do you think that the universe is large? It is nothing in comparison to the greatness of God. So you see, matter *matters* because of what it shows us about God.

In like manner, man-kind was created with the unique abilities of thought, emotion, and expression through language; for the purpose of having the capacities necessary for knowing, loving, and worshipping God. In other words, we (human beings) have been given everything that we need to *glorify* God. God created humans with all of the mental and emotional abilities that are necessary for recognizing the indescribable worth of God in His holiness, and responding to His indescribable worth and glory in loving adoration and worship of Him. For, God created people with the specific intent that of all the creatures in the universe, man would most clearly and intentionally glorify God, by reflecting, revealing, and making known His glory.

The new life that Christians are given in Christ is a life of knowing God, loving God, worshiping God, and thus, glorifying God. **Walking in newness of life is all about glorifying God.** The new life that Christ died to give His people is a life of knowing God, enjoying God, and being changed by God so that we become increasingly set apart (holy) to God. For God has said to His people, "You shall be holy, for I am holy" (1 Peter 1:16).

Our new life in Christ is exactly that: it is *a new life*. As we draw near to God and seek to know Him better, love Him more, serve Him more, and glory in Him only; He will change us - He will set us apart (make us holy) unto Himself, for His glory; for His purposes. He will do this by His own divine and sovereign power. He will accomplish all that He has set out to accomplish in and through us. For, the Bible tells us "In love, he predestined us for adoption as sons through Jesus Christ, according to the purpose of his will, to the praise of his glorious grace, with which he has blessed us in the Beloved..." And "...having been predestined according to the purpose of him who works all things according to the counsel of his will... ...we who were the first to hope in Christ might be to the praise of his glory" (See Ephesians 1:4-11, Philippians 2:13).

Since walking in newness of life is about glorifying God and becoming holy; walking in newness of life is about walking in the conscious reality of the awesome holiness of God, worshipping God, and being changed by the glorious reality of who God is. For, Christianity is all about God making people holy by drawing near to them and changing them into His Holy image - by allowing them to see the holiness of God in the person of Jesus Christ (Romans 8:28-29; 2 Corinthians 3:18). By walking (living life) in the conscious, worshipful awareness of the most holy, all-powerful, perfectly moral, exceedingly excellent, resplendent and glorious Divine Being (who is our Creator God and the Sustainer of our lives) we will naturally begin to live our lives in a different way than we do now. We will become progressively set-apart (holy) in all of our thinking, speaking, and behavior. Christianity is about divine transformation, not self-reformation.

In closing, the first step that anyone takes in walking in newness of life is a step of learning how to think about God in the right way. Today, we have begun to do this. We have considered the truth that God is holy (set-apart) in His self-existence, His moral perfections; His sovereignty, and in all of His other manifold perfect features.

We have learned that God's holiness makes Him glorious; deserving of our praise, adoration, and esteem. We have also learned that God created people with the intent that they would bring glory to Him. We have learned that God has provided us (humans) with everything that is needful for recognizing the glory of God, and thus, appropriately responding to Him in worship. We have also learned that by walking in the conscious, worshipful reality of God, He will begin to change us - by His own sovereign power and prerogative, and for His glory. We learned that Christianity is about divine transformation, not self-imposed acts of self-reformation.

So, if you want your life to change and you want to start walking in newness of life; all you have to do is meditate on who God is and think about the perfect moral nature of God (think about His holiness). Spend time thinking about what it means that God is eternal, having no beginning and no end. Ask yourself, "What does it mean that God is *'the LORD'* and *'there is no other God'?"* (Isaiah 45:5). Think about the fact that God is unrestricted and unlimited in His authority, dominion, and power (that He is sovereign). Consider what it means that God is holy, that God is perfectly good, that God is glorious, and that God created you with the unique abilities and capacities necessary for knowing God, loving God, worshiping God, and glorifying God. If you want to start walking in newness of life, remind yourself that even in this very moment, as you read these words, in heaven there are great and awesome - terrifyingly beautiful and powerful creatures crying out, day and night, one to another, *"Holy, holy, holy, is the Lord God Almighty, who was and is and is to come!"*

Day 2: Trusting in God

Trust in the LORD forever,
for the LORD GOD is an everlasting rock.
Isaiah 26:4

Trusting in God is a necessary means to the end of experiencing the many graces of walking in newness of life in Christ. Therefore, the second step that we take in walking in newness of life is the step of learning that we can trust God. God is the only sure foundation for our lives, and if we are going to walk in newness of life, we must know and believe (deep in our hearts) that we can always trust God. After all, our new life is completely dependent on the trustworthiness of God to change us and make us holy. Of course, we begin to know that we can trust God when we start to think about God in the right way (as we began to do in the last devotion). However, there is more to trusting God than simply acknowledging that He is real and that He is holy, even demons do that (Luke 4:33-34; James 2:19). Truly trusting God requires understanding both that God is the only person Who is always worthy of our trust, and understanding why God is the only person that is always worthy of our trust. Trusting God also requires understanding that we cannot even trust ourselves as much as we trust God. In this essay we will begin to step out in faith walking in newness of life, as we attempt to give a solid foundation for our feet to land on by meditating on trusting in God.

Often, women who have been disappointed by people that they have put their trust in, feel as though they cannot trust anyone, including God. Perhaps, you are one of those women. I use to be one of those women. If you are, then this Scripture may help you, as it once helped me: "God is not man, that he should lie, or a son of man, that he should change his mind. Has he said, and will he not do it? Or has he spoken, and will he not fulfill it?" (Numbers

23:19). That Scripture is very interesting, is it not? In it, we read that 'God is not a man that He should lie' - as if to say that all men lie. The Scripture also says that 'God is not a son of man, that He should change His mind' - as if to say all men change their minds. It is probably for these two reasons that, in John 2:24-25, we read about Jesus that He "… Did not trust himself unto them, for that he knew all men, and because he needed not that anyone should bear witness concerning man; for He Himself knew what was in man" (John 2:24-25). The Numbers passage above ends by asking a very good question regarding the trustworthiness of God: "Has he spoken, and will he not fulfill it?" Personally, I think that this question is the only question that matters when it comes to whether or not we can trust God. We must ask ourselves, "Has God always done what He said He would do?" If the answer to that question is no (which it, emphatically, is not) then we should not trust God. However, if the answer to that question is yes (which it, emphatically, is) then, **we must trust God.**

Sometimes, we may feel as though we cannot trust anyone except ourselves. However, we cannot even trust ourselves as much as we can trust God. After all, our hearts can deceive us. Sometimes, we believe what we want to believe because it is easier to believe a lie than it is to believe a painful truth. We often believe what we think needs to be true, depending on how we feel, and despite what we know to be true. For example, how many of us have ignored the obvious unfaithfulness of a friend, because we could not bear the thought of losing the friendship? In those cases, we ignore the truth to our own detriment; and thus prove that we cannot trust ourselves as much as we can trust God.

Furthermore, we cannot trust ourselves, as much as we can trust God because we are fallible. That we are *fallible means that we can make mistakes; that we are subject to error.* Sometimes we make mistakes out of blind or willful ignorance. At other times, we make an error in judgment because we, simply, do not know what is best;

for, as humans we are limited in our knowledge. We frequently mistake the motives or meanings of the words and actions of other people. And, often, our past situations and relationships obscure our ability to perceive our present realities (our relationships, situations, and circumstances) accurately. This is one reason that the Bible warns us that we cannot even trust our own hearts. God's word says, "The heart is deceitful above all things, and desperately sick; who can understand it?" (Jeremiah 17:9). Instead of trusting in our own hearts, we should learn to trust God to give us the wisdom that we need for all of the relationships, situations, and circumstances in our lives. We can trust God in all of these things because, unlike us, God is infallible (that is, *God is not capable of making mistakes or being wrong*).

You see, we can trust God in our relationships because God knows the hearts of all men. The Bible says, "...no creature is hidden from his sight, but all are naked and exposed to the eyes of him to whom we must give account" (Hebrews 4:13). Even the smartest woman in the world can never know the hearts of others. Quite a few women have deceived themselves into believing that they do know the hearts and minds of their husbands, children, and friends. Sometimes, I have heard women say things like, "I know what you were thinking!" or, "I know why you said that!" or "He would not admit it, but I knew that he really felt..." However, nobody truly knows what other people are thinking - only God knows what other people are thinking. We do not know the hearts, the motives, or the minds of others. (If we were truthful with ourselves, we might even admit that half the time we do not even know our own hearts, motives, and minds.) However, God does know the hearts, the motives, and the minds of all people. Therefore, we can trust God to lead us in all of our relationships.

Also, we can trust God to give us wisdom in every circumstance and decision in our lives. It is a foolish woman who thinks that she has enough understanding within herself to live life without asking

God for direction. For, no one (except God) knows how a decision, which is made today, will impact life tomorrow. Eve was the smartest woman in the world. She was perfect in every way. She had the perfect mind, the perfect body, the perfect marriage, and the perfect home. But, she messed it all up with one wrong decision. She is the first example that God gives to us in the Bible to teach us the lesson that we are not to trust in ourselves more than we trust God (Genesis 3). We should learn from our mother Eve, and always remember to trust God to give us the wisdom necessary to make every decision, which we must make.

In the same way, we can trust God to lead us in every circumstance of life in which we find ourselves. As the Lord said, "I will instruct you and teach you in the way you should go; I will counsel you with my eye upon you. Be not like a horse or a mule, without understanding, which must be curbed with bit and bridle, or it will not stay near you" (Psalm 32:8-9).

Ultimately, there are three main reasons that we can trust God in all of our relationships, situations, and circumstances. First, we can trust God because He knows everything. Second, we can trust God because He loves us perfectly. Finally, we can trust God because He is Holy.

First, we can trust God because He knows everything that there is to know. In other words, God is all-knowing. God knows everything about us. He knows everything about our pasts. He knows our present circumstances and He knows the outcome of every person's future. He knows what makes us tick (and He also knows what ticks us off). He knows what we think about everything in life. He knows every feeling that we have ever felt, and He knows every reason that we have ever felt those feelings. He knows what we think about life and what we think about death. More importantly, He knows everything that there truly is to know about both life and death. God knows all the wrongs that were committed against us and all the wrongs that we have committed against others. God knows us better than anyone else has ever known us, and He knows us better than anyone will ever know us. He even knows us better than we know ourselves. Remarkably, Jesus impressed the all-knowing ability of God on the hearts of His followers by saying, "Are not five sparrows sold for two pennies? And not one of them is forgotten before God. Why, even the hairs of your head are all numbered. Fear not; you are of more value than many sparrows" (Luke 12:6-7).

Secondly, we can trust God because He loves us. He does not love us because of anything that we have done. Therefore, we do not have to worry about undoing His love for us, for it is not possible for anything to undo the love of God. As the Scripture says, "…Neither death nor life, nor angels nor rulers, nor things present nor things to come, nor powers, nor height nor depth, nor anything else in all creation, will be able to separate us from the love of God in Christ Jesus our Lord (Romans 8: 38-39; See context in verses 31-39). You see, God loves us because "God is love" (1 John 4:16). God loves us with pure, undefiled, and incorruptible love. For this reason, we can be confident in the love of God. In other words, God has no hidden motives - so we never have to wonder what His angle is. Nor does God need anything from us; so we do not have to wonder if God is trying to manipulate us, or pull one over on us (Acts 17:25). Bottom line: we can trust God because He loves us with a perfect love.

Finally, we can trust God because God is holy. He only ever does the right thing. He can never sin. He never changes. He never lies. He is all knowing and all powerful; has unlimited wisdom, and He loves us with an unfailing love (James 1:13; Zephaniah 3:5; Hebrews 6:18). For all of these reasons and at least a million more reasons than these: we can trust God. Most importantly, God is worthy of our trust because He has never, ever failed to keep His Word. Whatever He has said He would do- He will do. He has always kept His word. He has always kept His commitments. And,

He always shows up at the exact time in which He should show up. For the Lord has said, "So shall my word be that goes out from my mouth; it shall not return to me empty, but it shall accomplish that which I purpose, and shall succeed in the thing for which I sent it" (Isaiah 55:11).

In closing, the second step that anyone takes in walking in newness of life is the step of learning that we can trust God. And, as you can see, we can trust God. We can trust Him more than we trust ourselves and more than we can trust anyone else. **God, Himself, is the sure foundation upon which we walk as we walk in newness of life.** We can confidently step out into the unknown world of holiness in Christ, because God is trustworthy. If you want to walk, unhindered, in newness of life, you will need to truly trust God. You will need to learn that you cannot trust in your own wisdom, your own past experiences, or even your own heart for direction and guidance in all of life's relationships, situations, and circumstances. Truly trusting God comes from knowing that God always does what He said He would do; He always has and He always will. The beautiful thing about this truth is that the longer that we walk with God, the easier it becomes to trust Him; because the longer that we walk with God, the more opportunities we have to grow in our personal knowledge of His absolute and perfect trustworthiness. Bottom line: walking in newness of life means trusting in God. Hence, the prophet Isaiah exhorts us (that is; he strongly encourages us and urges us), *"Trust in the LORD forever, for the LORD GOD is an everlasting rock."*

Day 3: A Lamp and a Light

Your word is a lamp to my feet and a light to my path.
Psalm 119:105

In Matthew 4:4, Jesus said, "Man shall not live by bread alone, but by every word that comes from the mouth of God." In a very real sense walking in newness of life is about learning how to live by every word that comes from the mouth of God. That is, walking in newness of life is about learning how to live by believing the Bible. We can trust the Bible because the Bible is God's Word, or as Jesus said, it comes from God's mouth. By saying that the Bible comes from God's mouth Jesus meant that all Scripture was breathed out by God; that it was inspired by Him. Second Timothy 3:16-17 confirms this by stating that "All Scripture is breathed out by God and profitable for teaching, for reproof, for correction, and for training in righteousness, that the man of God may be complete, equipped for every good work."

Unlike the Bible, other books are inspired or breathed out by men. They are, therefore, based on the words, research, and opinions of men. Since the words that fill those books come from men, their usefulness is limited by what men can know and what men can do. They are also limited by the truth that men understand and at times affected by the lies that men want to tell. But, the Word of God is not limited by any of those things, for God is not limited in His wisdom or knowledge, and He never lies (Colossians 2:2-3; Hebrews 6:18). This is why Jesus said that men shall not live by bread alone, but by every word that comes from the mouth of God. All this to say that we can trust the Word of God to teach us how to walk in newness of life.

The Holy Spirit is the One who inspired the Bible. In other words, the Holy Spirit is the one who carried the minds, hearts, and thoughts of the human agents that God used to pen the Words of the Holy Script; and He is also the One that shows us how we can rightly apply the Bible to our lives. For, it is the Holy Spirit that makes the Bible come alive to us when we read it. This is why Jesus said, "It is the Spirit who gives life; the flesh is no help at all. The words that I have spoken to you are spirit and life" (John 6:63). When a believer reads the Bible, the Holy Spirit of God causes the words that are read to make sense to her and gives her newness of life by the truth of them. The Holy Spirit is the One who both makes God's Word come alive to the believer and He also makes the believer come alive by God's Word.

First Corinthians 2:12-13 explains, "...Now we have received not the spirit of the world, but the Spirit who is from God, that we might understand the things freely given us by God. And we impart this in words not taught by human wisdom but taught by the Spirit, interpreting spiritual truths to those who are spiritual." Those who are spiritual are those who have been made spiritually alive in Christ, they are believers; they are Christians. The spiritual truths that this verse speaks of are the life-giving words of God that we can read in the Bible.

Hebrews 4:12 tells us "The word of God is alive and powerful. It is sharper than the sharpest two-edged sword, cutting between soul and spirit, between joint and marrow. It exposes our innermost thoughts and desires." The words alive and powerful in this verse teach us that God's word has the ability and the power to do things in our lives that the words of other books do not have the ability or power to do. For example, through the Bible, God reveals to us our inward motives and helps us to understand the roots of our wayward behaviors. The believer often finds that, through the Bible, God addresses concerns that we have never even shared with another person, concerns which we may never have even spoken out loud. For, the Word of God is the key that opens the hidden doors of the heart and releases the burdened soul from its prison of worry and anxiety. The Word of God is alive in that the Holy Spirit speaks the truth of God to us through it; it is powerful because by reading it God transforms us into the image of His Son (2 Corinthians 3:18; Colossians 3:9-10).

You see, the Bible is the book of God's self-revelation to man. If you want to know God, you must read the Bible. If you want to understand the truth about your life and the reason that you exist - you must read the Bible. For in the Bible, we learn to live in the way that God desires men (and women) to live. In it we learn about God, we learn about ourselves, and we learn everything that we need to learn about walking in newness of life. The Word of God makes known the ways of God and leads the believer in right paths (Psalm 25:4, 119:35); in it we receive clear directions for how we can live a holy and God-glorifying life. Through the divinely inspired words of Scripture the Holy Spirit of God warns us of how we can stay clear of treacherous paths, in which if we were to walk, we would become entangled with the weeds of sin. The Bible lights our paths and it is a lamp to our feet, so that we can walk in newness of life in this dark and fallen world. For this reason we must read and obey God's word every day.

Day 4: Entangling Sin

Let us also lay aside every encumbrance
and the sin which so easily entangles us,
and let us run with endurance the race that is set before us...
Hebrews 12:1

In the last devotion, we saw that the believer must read and obey the Bible. We saw that by reading and obeying the Bible, she will be kept safe from many of the evils that would keep her from walking in newness of life in Christ. One of the evils, which the Word of God warns believers about, is that they cannot walk in newness of life on treacherous paths that are entangled with the weeds of sin. In this devotion, we will try to clearly explain what sin is, why we do it, and how it entangles us. In this way, we will be better prepared for walking in newness of life, for we will understand why God commands that we stay off the treacherous paths covered with the entangling weeds of sin.

The word *sin means missing the mark; a fault, failure (in an ethical sense), a sinful deed.* From the Scripture, we know that sin consists of missing the mark of God's holiness. It is anything that we say, think, or do that is not holy - as God is Holy. Sin is any way in which people, who were created to be God's image bearers (Genesis 1:26-27), fail to reveal an accurate picture of who God is or fail to worship Him as God. In this way, sin is a suppression of the truth about God; a suppression of the truth about God's holiness; a suppression of the truth about God's glory. In fact, the Bible qualifies sin *as a falling short of God's glory*. All people have fallen short of God's glory. Even people that the Bible describes as 'blameless according to the law,' 'righteous,' and 'devout' (Luke 1:6; Philippians 3:3-6), are still sinners and are still in need of a Savior. The Scripture is clear, "... all have sinned and fall short of the glory of God" (Romans 3:23).

Acts of sin (sinful behaviors) consist of breaking the law of God and in not keeping the law of God. But, sin is more than what we do and what we do not do. Sin is a principle of rebellion at work within our mortal bodies, as well. It is a principle that the Bible describes as an evil lying close at hand- "...waging war against the law of my mind and making me captive..." (Romans 7:21-22, see context in verses 14-25). You see, sin is more than misdeeds, misdemeanors, and misconduct; it is a principle within each human being's flesh which is at war with God.

We are all born slaves to sin because we have inherited a sinful nature (i.e., the flesh) from the first man that was created- Adam (Romans 5:12-14, 18-19; 6:6, 20). When Adam disobeyed God, he died. In other words, when Adam sinned, his spirit; (the *spirit* meaning *the breath or the life principle in living beings)* was separated from God. God is *life* (Genesis 3:17; Deuteronomy 30:15-20, John 14:6; Colossians 3:4); therefore, to be separate from God is to be separate from life: **it is to be dead.**[3] Adam is the father of the human race and Adam's wife, Eve, is the mother of the human race; they are the "parents" of the entire human race (Genesis 3:20, 4: 1-2, 5:1-

---

[3]Adam's sin in the Garden resulted in a "first death" (of sorts) for the whole human race (Genesis 2:17; Hosea 6:7; Romans 5:12-21). This first death (in Adam) is the death that Christ conquered on the cross for His people (1 Corinthians 15:54-57; Hebrews 2:14-18). That is why Romans 5:17 says, "For if, because of one man's trespass, death reigned through that one man, much more will those who receive the abundance of grace and the free gift of righteousness reign in life through the one man Jesus Christ." And, likewise, in John 5:24 we read that Jesus said, "Truly, truly, I say to you, whoever hears my word and believes him who sent me has eternal life. He does not come into judgment, but *has passed from death to life"* (emphasis mine). When Jesus spoke of passing from death to life, He was talking about passing from the first death (that came to the human race as a result of Adam's sin); into eternal life. Eternal life is given to those that are reconciled (brought back into a right relationship) with God through Jesus' death, burial, and resurrection. In other words, Jesus was saying that those who heard and believed His words- would never experience the second death because they had already passed out of death and into life. That is, those who believe in Christ have life already because the separation between believers and God is completely destroyed in Christ. Hence, the Bible says that we are reconciled to God in Christ (2 Corinthians 5:18; Colossians 1:15-20). The Bible uses the term "second death" to describe the final, everlasting state in which the unsaved soul is permanently abandoned to its sinful existence separated from God in everlasting destruction in hell (Revelation 20:6, 14).

5). This means that all of our family trees have their roots in the union of Adam and Eve. And, therefore, we all share in their spiritual DNA. Since we have their spiritual DNA, we are all born corrupted by sin and under the judgment of God (Genesis 2:15-17; Psalm 51:5).[4] This is what Romans 5:12 is explaining where we read that, "… Sin came into the world through one man, and death through sin, and so death spread to all men because all sinned…"

All though we are born corrupted by sin and in spiritual death; we sin because we want to sin. For, the Bible teaches that it is our own desires that give birth to our sinful actions, "…desire when it has conceived gives birth to sin…" (James 1:15). In like manner, Ephesians 2: 1-2 says that we "… were dead in the trespasses and sins in which you [we] once walked, following the course of this world, following the prince of the power of the air, the spirit that is now at work in the sons of disobedience — among whom we all once lived in the passions of our flesh, carrying out the desires of the body…" In both of these verses, we learn that all of our wrong doing goes back to our own inner longings and personal desires. We naturally want to do what we think will most benefit ourselves, and we always choose in accordance with the strongest desire which we have at any given moment. We all want our own way, and our own way is almost always opposed to God's way. For, even when we want something that is good and right we usually want it for the wrong reasons. For example, we might want to be honest people, but we may want to be honest because it makes us feel good about ourselves, or because honesty is a trait that will make us look good to others. Or, maybe we want to be good mothers, but we may

---

4 Obviously, Jesus was not born corrupted by sin and under the judgment of God, for God is Jesus' Father- not Adam. We begin to see here, in our study on sin, the vital importance of the doctrines of the incarnation, the virgin birth, and the truth that God is Jesus' Father in a way that God is not every other human-being's Father (i.e. we begin to see why it matters that Jesus is *"the only begotten son of God, from the bosom of the Father"* John 1:18). Here are some verses for study in support of these doctrines: Genesis 3:15; Isaiah 7:14; Matthew 1:18-25; Luke 1:35; John 1:1-3, 14,18; 3:16; 5:17-18; Romans 1:1-4; and 1 John 4:9.

want to be a good mom just to prove our worth to ourselves or to another person. In both of those examples, we do not desire good behaviors because we love God with all of our hearts, souls, minds, or strength (Luke 10:27). In these examples, what we want is the right thing, but we want the right thing for the wrong reasons. For, we want them for our own benefit - not for God's glory. So, the prophet Isaiah was correct when He described the human sin-condition like this: "We are all infected and impure with sin. When we display our righteous deeds, they are nothing but filthy rags" (Isaiah 64:6, NLT).

Bottom line: We all sin and our sin kills everything that it touches. Sin warps, twists, and deceives human beings. Our sin natures cannot be satisfied, will not be quieted, and they never have enough. Sin hates everything good and desires everything evil. Sin robs innocence, assaults virtue, and betrays fidelity. Sin desecrates, destroys, and ravages the human soul. Sin is a deadly parasite feeding off of every human being; it is the death nail in every coffin, and it is most truly the festering infection of all fallen flesh. Sin rages against God's authority, disdains the thought of submitting to the life-giving law of Christ, and subverts the purpose of God in humanity: to glorify His great name. For this reason, when we sin and when we are sinned against, we experience death in all of its various forms of spiritual, emotional, mental, and relational brokenness. It is like James 1:15 says, "...desire when it has conceived gives birth to sin, and sin when it is fully grown brings forth death." Therefore, we must do everything that we can to avoid the treacherous paths of life which are entangled with weeds of sin. And, at all costs, we must "...also lay aside every encumbrance and the sin which so easily entangles us, and let us run with endurance the race that is set before us..."

Day 5: Merciful Roadblocks

Since, therefore, we have now been justified by his blood, much more
shall we be saved by him from the wrath of God. Romans 5:9

God does not take kindly to people who ignore Him; actually, He hates them (Psalm 5:5; 11:5). Ignoring God is a violent assault against the majesty and glory of who God is. It is wrong to pretend that God does not exist (Romans 1:18-32). It is an affront to God to pay no heed to His glorious holiness. It is a hostile thing in the eyes of God that men prefer to drown in the sewage pipes of human sin; rather than swim in the clean, refreshing ocean of the glory of God. For, God is jealous for His people; God is jealous for His glory (Exodus 20:5; 34:14). Truly, God hates all sin, and God is wrathful towards all sinners. As Nahum 1:2 says, "The LORD is a jealous and avenging God; the LORD is avenging and wrathful; the LORD takes vengeance on his adversaries and keeps wrath for his enemies" (Nahum 1:2).

God's wrath is a violent reaction that God's holiness (His set apart, morally perfect nature) has to sin. The cross helps us understand how terrifyingly violent God's wrathful reaction to sin is. We know from Isaiah 53:10 that the crucifixion of Jesus Christ was ordained by God for an acceptable payment for our sins; for it says, "...it was the will of the Lord to crush him; he has put him to grief." The description of what Jesus looked like after He was crushed by God for the payment of sin gives us some idea of God's deep hatred for and offense at the sin of His people. The Bible says that when Jesus was crucified He was "...marred, beyond human semblance and his form beyond that of the children of mankind..." (Isaiah 52:14). Jesus' death reveals how real and how powerful the wrath of God is. His death also reveals how significant and important God's holiness is, for it was on the cross that Jesus fully and completely bore the holy wrath of God on behalf of His people.

Hell is a place where God's hatred at sin, and His wrath towards sinners is expressed. Hell is a place where unrepentant sinners will suffer the just consequences for having not valued the holiness, glory, and beauty of God during their earthly lives. Hell is a place that God has designed for everlasting judgment. Hell is promised to be a place of perfect justice. Jesus believed in hell and so should we. He warned people, "Don't be afraid of those who want to kill your body; they cannot touch your soul. Fear only God, who can destroy both soul and body in hell" (Matthew 10:28, NLT), and He described hell as a place "...Where the maggots never die, and the fire never goes out..." (Mark 9:48, NLT).

Romans 1:18 says, "...the wrath of God is revealed from heaven against all ungodliness and unrighteousness of men, who by their unrighteousness suppress the truth." From this verse we learn that God's wrath is a present tense reality for man-kind. In other words, we see here that even now (i.e., in this life-time, on this planet, and not just in the future in hell) God's wrath is being revealed from heaven against all the ungodliness and unrighteousness of people - who are suppressing the truth about God. In fact, this is the very reason why Paul says that He is not ashamed of the Gospel. Paul says that it is the Gospel (the good news about Jesus' atoning cross work) that saves people from God's wrath. He said, "...For I am not ashamed of the gospel, for it is the power of God for salvation to everyone who believes, to the Jew first and also to the Greek." (Romans 1:17). You see, it is through faith in the message of the Gospel that God saves us from His wrath.

So then the question is, "*What is the expression of God's wrath in this life time?*" In other words, "*What does the Bible mean where it says that that 'the wrath of God is revealed from heaven against all ungodliness and unrighteousness of men'?*" The answer to that question may surprise you. Most people that believe in the wrath of God think that His wrath is expressed here on earth primarily in the form of tsunamis, earth quakes, and in massive large scale devastations. And, to some degree that assumption is not entirely false. However, those types of catastrophes are more like the birth pains of creation, as it awaits its liberation day when God vindicates His holiness at the end of time by redeeming His people and judging the unsaved. Actually, the primary expression of God's wrath in this life-time is more subtle than world-wide calamity.

God reveals His wrath from heaven in this age by handing sinners over to an increasing fulfillment of their own sinful lusts. Another way to say that is to say God primarily expresses His wrath at this time in history by allowing sinners to gratify their own sinful desires more and more. In a sense, to be under the wrath of God is to be allowed to do the very things that we most desire to do: ignore God and have a hay-day with our pet sins. Some might think that this sounds great. But, it is more like hell on earth to be left to our own sinful longings, abandoned to our rebellion against God, and given up to the corrosive lusts of our flesh. Even so, God doesn't give the "children of wrath" (Ephesians 2:3) anything other than what they want. As one Bible teacher said, "The essence of God's action in wrath is to *give men what they choose*, in all its implications: nothing more, and equally nothing less."[5]

That abandonment to one's own base and ungodly desires is what the Bible is talking about in Romans 1 where it says, "For the wrath of God is revealed from heaven against all ungodliness and unrighteousness of men, who by their unrighteousness suppress the truth..." (v.18); "Therefore God gave them up in the lusts of their hearts to impurity," (v.24), "For this reason God gave them up to dishonorable passions..." (v.26), "And since they did not see fit to acknowledge God, God gave them up to a debased mind to do what ought not to be done" (v.28). We can see in this passage the perfect justness of God's judgment in wrath. God reveals Himself

---

[5] Packer, J.I. 1993. *Knowing God.* Downers Grove, Illinois: Inter Varsity Press. 153.

to people and when they do not want to acknowledge Him, because they would rather satiate themselves with sin; He lets them have more of what they want: more sin and more self-destruction.

Therefore, when we are caught in our sin or we get in trouble for wrong doing - we should view it as a merciful roadblock that is keeping us off the paths that lead to hell. We should be thankful to God when He keeps us from sin. Roadblocks on the paths of life are one proof that God has not completely abandoned us to our sinful lusts. When He sets up a road block on our sinful paths to hell, He is showing us mercy and love. When he stops us in our sinful tracks, God is withholding His wrath from us temporarily in the hope that we will turn away from our sin, and seek God's mercy by asking for His forgiveness, and trusting in Christ for salvation. When God allows our wrong doing to catch up with us (here on earth), He is giving us an opportunity to escape the ultimate expression of His wrath in Hell.

It is a mercy from God to get caught in wrong doing, and it is also a mercy to feel a sense of conviction for our sins against God. If we do not ever feel convicted for our sins, we will never seek God for saving mercy, for His forgiveness. We all sin by not loving and worshipping God. For that reason, we are all under God's wrath and in need of His forgiveness through Christ. If we are going to escape God's wrath in this life and escape God's wrath in Hell, we must seek the mercy and forgiveness of God by clinging to the only hope that we have: the shed blood of Jesus Christ. For, when we receive God's forgiveness and mercy in Christ, we are set right with God, we are justified in His sight. And the Scripture promises that if we are "…justified by his blood, much more shall we be saved by him from the wrath of God."

Day 6: The Power of God

The message of the cross is
foolish to those who are headed for destruction!
But we who are being saved know it is the very power of God.
1 Corinthians 1:18, NLT

The message of the cross (spoken of in the verse above) is the message "...that Christ died for our sins in accordance with the Scriptures, that he was buried, that he was raised on the third day in accordance with the Scriptures..." (1 Corinthians 15:3-4). In other words, the message of the cross is the message that in the crucifixion, Jesus took upon Himself - in His body - all of our sin, so that by shedding His blood on the cross, He could make *atonement* (full payment) for our sins by bearing the full brunt of the wrath of God on our behalf (Hebrews 9:22). After Christ had died on our behalf, He was buried, and then He rose from the dead. The message of the cross is the power of God, because it is through faith in this message that God saves His people from their sin.

God saves us through the word of the cross by making our salvation completely dependent on the atoning cross-work of Jesus. To receive salvation, we need only turn towards the Lord in faith, admitting our need for salvation; and trusting in Christ's death as sufficient for providing a full payment for our sins. For the Word says, "...everyone who calls upon the name of the Lord shall be saved" (Acts 2:21). In this way, God makes our salvation dependent on *His* mercy and grace; as opposed to our salvation being dependent on own efforts. That is, God makes our salvation dependent on *His power*; as opposed to making our salvation dependent on *our power*. Hence, Scripture says, "The message of the cross... .....is the very power of God" (1 Corinthians 1:18, NLT).

The word of the cross is the power of God *to us who are being saved* because believers understand that we have no power to save ourselves; i.e., we understand that only God can save us from our sin, death, and His wrath. This is very good news for powerless people; we who are weak, frail, and sinful rejoice in the knowledge that God saves "…Not by might, nor by power, but by my [God's] Spirit" (Zachariah 4:6). God chose to save the weaklings, the messed up people, and the poor people of this world to be the only ones who receive His free gift of salvation through faith in Jesus' cross-work. As Jesus said, "Those who are well have no need of a physician, but those who are sick. I have not come to call the righteous, but sinners to repentance" (Luke 5:31-32). We who are weak and beggarly rejoice that God saves sinners by His own gracious will and power; and not by the efforts, merits, and good-works of our own doing.

Again, **God only saves sinful, weak, and morally bankrupt people.** In doing this, He shows the created order His manifold wisdom. He does this by saving undeserving, helpless sinners and then transforming them by His own power into the holy servants of God (Ephesians 3:7-11). Most of all, He magnifies His grace by making salvation a gift that is not earned - but, instead, one that is freely given to the humble recipients of His favor (Ephesians 2:4-10). In making salvation a free-gift received by the humble, God puts the so called self-righteous and the successful people of this world in their proper place: to shame for their self-righteous pride. That's the point of 1 Corinthians 1:26-29 which says, "Remember, dear brothers and sisters, that few of you were wise in the world's eyes or powerful or wealthy when God called you. Instead, God chose things the world considers foolish in order to shame those who think they are wise. And he chose things that are powerless to shame those who are powerful. God chose things despised by the world; things counted as nothing at all, and used them to bring to nothing what the world considers important. As a result, no one can ever boast in the presence of God" (NLT).

First Corinthians 1:18 says that the message of the cross is the power of God *to those that are being saved*. Those who *are being saved* are those who are daily experiencing God's resurrection-power in their lives; not those who just say that they believe the gospel message. There are some people who think that they are in the group of those who are *being saved*, but they have no real relationship with Jesus Christ; they have no personal experiential knowledge of the power of the cross to save them from sin. The Word of God warns us about these people saying, "They will act religious, but they will reject the power that could make them godly." And also warns us, "Stay away from people like that" (2 Timothy 3:5, NLT).

People that think they are *being saved*, and yet, never seem to experience any of the fruit of saving faith (conviction over wrong-doing, hunger for God, love for God, joy in God, a desire to be with other Christians, etc. etc.); are self-deceived: **they are not really being saved.** People who are being saved experience the power of the cross of Christ to save them from sin's power every day - not just judgment day. Unfortunately, there are some people that do not even realize that they do not know God (Matthew 7:21-23, 25:31-46).

For this reason, we need to check the quality of our professing faith against the fruit of salvation in our lives. We can do this by comparing our lives with the Biblical description of what the Christian life is supposed to be like. We can ask ourselves Bible-based questions that help us measure the genuineness of our faith by the objective standard of God's Word. For example, we can ask ourselves questions like: are we sinning less than before we came to faith in Christ? Do we feel conviction when we do sin? Do we want to obey God's word? Do we even want to read God's Word? Do we love God more than we love ourselves? Do we find joy in God? Do we want to be with other people who find their joy in God? All this to say, we must obey the admonition of Scripture, "Examine yourselves, to see whether you are in the faith. Test yourselves. Or do you not realize this about yourselves, that Jesus Christ is in you?—unless indeed you fail to meet the test!" (2 Corinthians 13:5).

None of us should foolishly buy into the false belief that salvation from sin is accomplished because we give verbal assent to the truth of the Bible. Even demons do that! James 2:19 says, "You believe that God is one; you do well. Even the demons believe—and shudder!" Real Christians - those who are being saved - experience the power of the cross to save them from sin more and more every day of their lives. We experience God's power in *real-time* as God destroys our deadly sin patterns and gives us new life through our relationship with Jesus. We experience God's power through the message of the cross every time that we are kept from fulfilling our sinful desires, we are enabled to deal with our messed up pasts, or we receive God's grace to accept our own frailties, and love others despite their frailties. The power of the cross is a present-tense reality; it is not just a future hope. For the power of the cross is the power of God to put us on a new path, walking in newness of life. The longer that we walk on that new path, the more we will experientially know that, to those of us who are being saved, **the message of the cross really is the very power of God.**

.

Day 7: The Narrow Path

For godly grief produces a repentance that leads to salvation
without regret, whereas worldly grief produces death.
2 Corinthians 7:10.

As we experience more and more of the goodness of God in our relationship with Him, we are naturally led into deeper and deeper levels of holiness. For, the kindness that we experience in our relationship with God produces in His children a godly grief in our souls, which leads us to confess and repent of more and more of our sin. As we do this we become holier; thus we begin to live in the joyful freedom of walking in newness of life.

Another way to say the same thing is to say *that the kindness of God causes us to feel a good-guilt over our wrongdoing.* Good-guilt is rooted in an awareness of the goodness and love that God has shown to His children. *Good-guilt* is *good* because it makes us want to turn away from the things in our lives that displease God (i.e., our sin) and turn towards the Lord Jesus Christ for the salvation that He died to give us. That is why the Scripture says, "Don't you see how wonderfully kind, tolerant, and patient God is with you? Does this mean nothing to you? Can't you see that his kindness is intended to turn you from your sin?" (Romans 2:4, NLT).

When we say that we repent of our sin we mean that we have *a change of mind about our sin; and for that reason, we turn away from our sin and towards God in the desire to live a God-glorifying life.* In other words, to repent of sin is to turn around and go in the opposite direction when we realize that we are heading the wrong way on the path of life. Repentance is the authenticating mark of our profession of faith in Christ. It is the first outward proof that we possess true saving faith. If we agree with God that our sin is wrong, we will do everything that we can to turn away from it and turn towards the righteousness that is ours because of the cross-work of Jesus Christ. It is in this way that repentance leads to salvation. As Isaiah 30:15a says, "In repentance and rest is your salvation, in quietness and trust is your strength..." (NIV).

In Luke 3:8, John the Baptist commands that the true children of God "Bear fruits in keeping with repentance." One fruit that is in keeping with repentance is confession of our sin. *Confession consists of giving full consent to, being in out-and-out agreement with, admitting wrongdoing, or an acknowledgement of debts owed.* That is, confession is the verbal expression of our agreement with God that He is correct (He is right) about the matter of our sin. In practical terms, this includes fully agreeing with God that our wrong attitudes, self-consumed motives, ungodly actions, destructive addictions, and immoral relationships are sinful. Confession also includes acknowledging that the sin-debt that we owe to God is beyond our ability to pay back. In short, confession is how we say, "Lord, You are right. I am walking on the wrong path. I am going in the wrong direction with my life. If You do not save me, I cannot be saved. Please, Lord, turn me around so that I am going in the right direction on the path that leads to life."

Confession of sin is an on-going practice in the life of every believer. It is a necessary part of maintaining fellowship with God. All believers continually struggle with sin in one form or another. Therefore, all believers must make a continual practice of confessing their sins to God. When we confess our sin, we can be sure that God will forgive us and that He will give us the grace to overcome our sinful habits. For the Word of God says, "If we confess our sins, He is faithful and just to forgive us our sins and to cleanse us from all unrighteousness" (1 John 1:9).

Confession is the authenticating mark of repentance, and likewise, repentance is the authenticating mark of our confession. They are like two sides of the same coin. If we truly agree with God about our sin, we will make every effort to stop sinning. We will do everything that we can do to turn away from our sin and turn towards God in the pursuit of holiness. Confession without turning away from sin is not real confession: it is lip-service that we are making to God. Giving lip-service to God reveals either deep stupidity (for who is stupid enough to play games with God?), or it reveals a genuine lack of understanding of who the God of the Bible is and how dangerous sin is. Jesus tells people who think that they are all set with half-hearted Christian living (things like insincere confession or lives that lack the fruits of repentance): "Those whom I love, I reprove and discipline, so be zealous and repent" (Revelation 3:19).

Repentance and confession reveal the presence of saving faith. If we truly believe that Jesus died for our sins, we will want to confess our sin and turn away from it. As the Apostle James said, "...the body apart from the spirit is dead, so also faith apart from works is dead" (James 2:26). In turning away from our sin by repenting of it, and in turning towards God in confession of our sin, we do the works that prove we possess saving-faith. Conversely, if we consistently choose to hide our sin and try to avoid the acts of confession and repentance we do the works that prove that we do not possess saving faith. If the latter is true of us, we can only expect judgment and discipline from God. For Proverbs 28:13 warns us, "Whoever conceals his transgressions will not prosper, but he who confesses and forsakes them will obtain mercy."

When we confess our sin; we should name the exact times that we have committed our pet sins, the precise places that we are more likely to indulge our sinful appetites, and the people with whom we feel the freest and most comfortable committing our sin. If we do this we will be helped in our repentance; for we will be more aware of the relationships, places, and opportunities in our lives that we must be careful to turn away from in repentance. Also, by being specific in our confession, we own more truthfully the provisions that we have made for committing our sins in the past. This level of honesty with God and ourselves will likely aid in the production of the good-guilt, i.e., the godly grief, over our sin that is appropriate for a believer to feel. Feeling godly grief will cause us to confess and repent of our sin more and more; making us holier and leading us into deeper and deeper levels of holiness. Confession and repentance of sin keeps us on the path that leads to salvation. Ongoing confession and repentance of sin will keep us on the narrow path that leads to life. That is why the Scripture says, "...godly grief produces a repentance that leads to salvation."

Day 8: Union with Christ

Since you have been raised to new life with Christ, set your sights on the realities of heaven, where Christ sits in the place of honor at God's right hand. Think about the things of heaven, not the things of earth. For you died to this life, and your real life is hidden with Christ in God. And when Christ, who is your life, is revealed to the whole world, you will share in all his glory.

Colossians 3:1-4, NLT

We receive the ability to walk in newness of life by being united to Christ in His death, burial, and resurrection. In the Bible when we read the little phrases 'in Christ', 'by Christ', 'with Christ', and 'through Christ' we are reading about the union that believers have with Christ. **God has given us everything that we need for walking in newness of life through our union with Christ.** For this reason, our union with Christ is very important to understand as we endeavor to live the Christian life in a way that will glorify God and honor Christ our King.

Our union with Christ began when God the Holy Spirit *baptized us (that is, He submerged us)* into the spiritual body of Jesus Christ (1 Corinthians 12:12-13). The moment that we were united to Christ, His death, burial, and resurrection took effect in our souls, and we were "…raised from the dead…" (spiritually speaking), so that we "….might walk in newness of life" (Romans 6:4). Christ had already paid for our sins many hundreds of years ago on a Roman cross. Therefore, when we were united to Christ through our faith in His cross work, our sin and spiritual death was left in the burial-tomb of Christ, and we were supernaturally raised up from death to life in Christ. That is why Colossians 3:1-4 says, "Since you have been raised to new life with Christ, set your sights on the realities of heaven, where Christ sits in the place of honor at God's right hand. Think about the things of heaven, not the things of earth. For you died to this life, and your real life is hidden with Christ in God. And when Christ, who is your life, is revealed to the whole world, you will share in all his glory" (NLT).

When we were united to Christ, we were born again. Jesus told a man once that, "…unless one is born again he cannot see the kingdom of God… …unless one is born of water and the Spirit, he cannot enter the kingdom of God. That which is born of the flesh is flesh, and that which is born of the Spirit is spirit" (John 3:3-7). You see, when the Holy Spirit baptized us into the spiritual body of Christ He was giving birth to us, He was giving us new-life in Christ. The more technical term for being born-again is the term *regeneration*. In Titus 3:4-7 we see the Apostle explain that regeneration is a work of the Holy Spirit of God, accomplished in the person of Jesus Christ, by the will of God. It says, "…when the *goodness and loving kindness of God our Savior appeared, he saved us,* not because of works done by us in righteousness, but *according to his own mercy,* by *the washing of regeneration and renewal of the Holy Spirit,* whom *he poured out on us richly through Jesus Christ our Savior,* so that being justified by his grace we might become heirs according to the hope of eternal life." (Emphasis mine.) It is because we have been united to Christ that we were cleansed from our sin, born-again, raised from the dead, and raised to walk in newness of life.

Through our union with Christ we have been adopted by God. In Ephesians 1:5-6, we read: "In love, he [God] predestined us for adoption as sons through Jesus Christ, according to the purpose of his will to the praise of his glorious grace, with which he has blessed us in the Beloved." This means that those of us who have believed in Jesus for the forgiveness of our sins have not only been saved from sin, death, God's wrath, and hell, but we have also been chosen by God to be His adopted children. John 1:12-13 explains that "…to all who did receive him [Christ], who believed in his name, he gave the right to become children of God, who were born, not of blood nor the will of the flesh nor of the will of man, but of God."

Peter tells us that through our union with Jesus we "...become partakers of the divine nature..." (2 Peter 1:3-4). We see here that in becoming one with Christ in our spirits we have been given the ability to participate in the nature of God. The ability to participate in the divine nature of God comes through His indwelling Holy Spirit (John 14:18-26; 2 Corinthians 3:18; Ephesians 1:13-14). In this way, we are new creatures, created in the image of Christ (Colossians 3:10). As 2 Corinthians 5:17 says, "Therefore, if anyone is in Christ, he is a new creation. The old has passed away; behold, the new has come"

Since we are new creatures that participate in the divine nature of God; our former relationship with sin has ended. It died and got buried in ancient Israel through our union with Christ. Therefore, in Christ, we are no longer ruled, governed, or enslaved by our sin. This is why the Word says, "We know that our old self was crucified with him in order that the body of sin might be brought to nothing, so that we would no longer be enslaved to sin, *for one who has died has been set free from sin*" (Romans 6:6-7, emphasis mine). So it is, by making us one with Christ, God released us from our enslavement to sin. Through our union with Christ, we are set free from sin so that we can serve God in righteousness. The Bible teaches this by saying, "For when you were slaves of sin, you were free in regard to righteousness. But what fruit were you getting at that time from the things of which you are now ashamed? For the end of those things is death. But now that you have been set free from sin and have become slaves of God, the fruit you get leads to sanctification and its end, eternal life. For the wages of sin is death, but the free gift of God is eternal life in Christ Jesus our Lord" (Romans 6:20-23).

Sin no longer has power over us because, through our union with Christ, God no longer requires us to obey His laws perfectly in order to be saved. The Word of God tells us, "...Christ is the end of the law for righteousness to everyone who believes" (Romans 10:4). We only need to trust in Christ and His atoning cross-work to be saved by God and for God to count us as righteous (i.e., just, approved by God). For in His earthly sojourn Christ perfectly obeyed all of the laws of God, and since we are one with Christ, God counts Christ's obedience to His law (the written code of the Old Testament Scriptures) as our obedience to His law. In this way, God credits us with Christ's righteousness (See, 2 Corinthians 5:21). This is what Romans 8:2-4 is talking about where the Word says; "...the law of the Spirit of life has set you [us] free in Christ Jesus from the law of sin and death. For God has done what the law, weakened by the flesh, could not do. By sending his own Son in the likeness of sinful flesh and for sin, he condemned sin in the flesh, in order that the righteous requirement of the law might be fulfilled in us, who walk not according to the flesh but according to the Spirit." (Romans 8:2-4).

Through our union with Christ, we are set free to serve God by living life with a simple, humble dependency on God. As Paul admonished the Galatian believers, "But I say, walk by the Spirit, and you will not gratify the desires of the flesh. ...If you are led by the Spirit, you are not under the law... ...the fruit of the Spirit is love, joy, peace, patience, kindness, goodness, faithfulness, gentleness, self-control; against such things there is no law" (Galatians 5:16-23). The Holy Spirit is inside of us, (i.e., believers in Christ), leading us, guiding us, and directing us in right paths that are pleasing to God. To walk in the Spirit means that we keep following the direction, guidance, and leading of His Holy Spirit. And, God has told us the fruit of the Spirit (the characteristics of His Spirit) so that we can discern the voice of the Spirit as we endeavor to follow His lead. If we always walk in the Spirit, we have no need to worry about displeasing God, for the Spirit of God will only ever lead us in ways that will fulfill the law of God. And, when we do break the law of God (because of our remaining sin or because of our ignorance of His Word), we do not need to worry. For the Bible says, "My dear children, I am writing this to you so that you will not sin. But if anyone does sin, we have an advocate who pleads our case before the Father. He is Jesus Christ, the one who is truly righteous" (1 John 2:1, NLT).

Even before God created the world, God decided that salvation and all that is needed to accomplish salvation would be freely given to His people by making them one with Christ in the obedience of His earthly life, His cross-death, His burial, and His resurrection (Ephesians 1: 4-6). Through our union with Christ, we are set free from sin's power, and we have been delivered from death. Through our union with Christ, we have been rescued from God's wrath and given a new nature. Through our union with Christ, we are released from law-keeping for the sake of salvation. Now through the indwelling Spirit of Christ, we only need to rely on the Holy Spirit of Christ in order to please God. Through our union with Christ we have been blessed with every spiritual blessing in Christ (Ephesians 1:3). This includes forgiveness for all of our sins, the righteousness of Christ, holiness, eternal life, and everything else that we need for walking in newness of life. For this reason, Paul wrote, "Since you have been raised to new life with Christ, set your sights on the realities of heaven, where Christ sits in the place of honor at God's right hand. Think about the things of heaven, not the things of earth. For you died to this life, and your real life is hidden with Christ in God. And when Christ, who is your life, is revealed to the whole world, you will share in all his glory. "

Day 9: An Inheritance of Grace

Therefore, preparing your minds for action, and being sober-minded,
set your hope fully on the grace that will be brought to you at the
revelation of Jesus Christ. 1 Peter 1:13

Scripture tells us that God loves His children. As the Apostle wrote, "See how very much our Father loves us, for he calls us his children, and that is what we are!" (1 John 3:1, NLT). Since God loves us He has rescued us from the "…kingdom of darkness and transferred us into the Kingdom of his dear Son, who purchased our freedom and forgave our sins" (Colossians 1:13; NLT). When God rescued us from our sin, He set us free from the ruling authority of Satan, and gave us His own Holy Spirit to dwell within us and teach us what it means to be the children of God. Romans 8:14-17 tells us "…For all who are led by the Spirit of God are sons of God. For you did not receive the spirit of slavery to fall back into fear, but you have received the Spirit of adoption as sons, by whom we cry, "Abba! Father!" The Spirit himself bears witness with our spirit that we are children of God, and if children, then heirs—heirs of God and fellow heirs with Christ, provided we suffer with him in order that we may also be glorified with him." In another place, we read that the Holy Spirit is "…the guarantee of our inheritance until we acquire possession of it, to the praise of his glory" (Ephesians 1:14, see also 2 Corinthians 1:22). And, Galatians 4:6-7 tells us that, "…God has sent the Spirit of his Son into our hearts, crying, "Abba! Father!" So you are no longer a slave, but a son, and if a son, then an heir through God." All this to say that as God's children we have become heirs who have been appointed a share in the immeasurable grace of God. Hence, we have been given *an inheritance of grace.*

Grace is the free, undeserved favor of God. Everything that we have in the Christian life we have received by God's grace. For, our God is the God of all grace (1 Peter 5:10); who sits on the throne of grace (Hebrews 4:16). Jesus Christ came to us full of grace and from Him we receive grace upon grace (John 1:14, 16). The gospel is preached to us by God's grace (Titus 2:11-14).We are saved by God's grace (Ephesians 2:5-8). We stand in God's grace (Romans 5:1-2). We are strengthened by God's grace (2 Corinthians 12:9). We are waiting for the grace that we will receive when we see Jesus face to face (1 Peter 1:13). Everything that the Christian has she has "…because of the grace of God that was given… in Christ Jesus" (1 Corinthians 1:4). I could go on, but I think that you can see where we are going with this: we are undeserving sinners, and yet we have been freely given an inheritance of Grace.

God has graciously made His children "co-heirs" with Christ. The Word says, "In Him we have obtained an inheritance…" (Ephesians 1:11).   The Bible tells us that our inheritance is "…imperishable, undefiled, and unfading, kept in heaven for you…" (1 Peter 1:4). In fact, Psalm 119:57 says, "*The LORD is my inheritance…"* (ISV), and Psalm 16:5-6 puts it like this: "The Lord is my chosen portion and my cup; you hold my lot. The lines have fallen for me in pleasant places; indeed, I have a beautiful inheritance." The inheritance of grace that we have received from our Heavenly Father includes everything from eternal life on the new earth to everlasting joy in the presence of God; and then, everything in between those two extremes, as well. We know that our inheritance includes all of this because the Bible tells us that, "…all things are yours… …the world or life or death or the present or the future—all are yours, and you are Christ's, and Christ is God's" (1 Corinthians 3:21-23 See also; Psalm 16:11; John 3:36; 2 Peter 3:8-14).

All though we have such a great inheritance that awaits us, the Bible warns us that God's children will suffer in this life. There are two main reasons for our suffering. The first cause of suffering in the Christian life is that God chose to leave His children with remaining sin. He did this so that we can be practiced in our dependence on God for living a holy life. At times resisting the urge to sin and gratify our lusts will result in suffering. Saying 'no' to the power of sin is hard work, but it is worth it, for Ephesians 5:5 warns us that we "… may be sure of this, that everyone who is sexually immoral or impure, or who is covetous (that is, an idolater), has no inheritance in the kingdom of Christ and God." Thankfully, God promised us an inheritance to help motivate us to live a holy life - even when it hurts us to do so

The second reason that the children of God will suffer is that we still live in a world that is ruled by Satan. Satan is God's enemy and, therefore, he is also the enemy of God's children. Satan hates God; he despises God's authority, and he is bitterly jealous of God's glory. In a similar way, the devil hates and despises God's children. The devil is full of rage towards us for many reasons. He hates us because we have been rescued from his power, and we have come under God's authority (Romans 6:22; Ephesians 2:1-9; Hebrews 2:14-15). He hates that we have Christ's Holy Spirit dwelling in us. He hates that we have become "...partakers of the divine nature (2 Peter 1:3-4). And, he especially hates that we have Christ in us "...the hope of glory" (Colossians 1:27). The devil will use everything in the world to try to make us forget the promise of God that we have a glorious inheritance waiting for us in heaven. However, God wants us to hold on to the hope of our inheritance, so that we are strengthened to resist the devil (James 4:7); even if resisting the devil and his power may cause us to suffer in this life. For this reason, the Scripture repeatedly warns us, "Do you not know the unrighteous will not inherit the kingdom of God… Do not be deceived: neither the sexually immoral, nor idolaters, nor adulterers, nor men who practice homosexuality, nor thieves, nor the greedy, nor drunkards, nor revilers, nor swindlers will inherit the kingdom of God" (1 Corinthians 6:9-10).

God chose us to be His adopted children. That is, God has rescued us from our sin and from the power of Satan by adopting us and making us His very own beloved children. As such, we have been given an undefiled, incorruptible inheritance of grace. Our inheritance is waiting for us in heaven. He has given us this hope to strengthen us in our obedience to Him, and to motivate us to resist the enemy of our souls. As we walk in newness of life, God has given us a place to fix our eyes, so that we don't wonder off the path of salvation. The inheritance of grace that God has promised us in Christ Jesus is our motivation to *walk a straight line* (so to speak). Our inheritance is our motivation to follow hard after God, even when following God is hard to do. That is why Scripture exhorts us by saying, "Therefore, preparing your minds for action, and being sober-minded, set your hope fully on the grace that will be brought to you at the revelation of Jesus Christ."

Day 10: A New Lease on Life

By his divine power, God has given us everything we need for living a godly life. We have received all of this by coming to know him, the one who called us to himself by means of his marvelous glory and excellence.
2 Peter 1:3-4, NLT

When God gave us newness of life through our union with Christ, He gave us a new purpose for living, a new home in heaven, a clean slate in life (that is, a clean conscience), a new heart with new desires, and a new relationship with God's law. That is what the Bible is talking about where it says, "By his divine power, God has given us everything we need for living a godly life. We have received all of this by coming to know him, the one who called us to himself by means of his marvelous glory and excellence" (2 Peter 1:3, NLT). In other words, God has not only given us a new life - *He has given us a whole new lease on life.*

Our new lease on life started with the new hearts that God gave us. In the Old Testament we read that God said, "… I will give you a new heart… I will take out your stony, stubborn heart and give you a tender, responsive heart" (Ezekiel 36:26, NLT). The Lord does not mean here that He is going to give us a new physical heart. Any old heart surgeon could do that. No, the new heart that God gives to His children is a heart that only God can give: a new spiritual heart. It is the heart of our souls; the thinking and feeling part of our being; the part of us that has desires and motivates us to act. The new heart that God gives us enables us to live in accord with God's will for our lives and obey the Law of Christ. Before we received these new hearts from the Lord, we could not have obeyed God if we had wanted to, but now the Bible says that we have become "…obedient from the heart…" (Romans 6:17). The old Testament describes our new heart obedience by saying that God has written His law on our hearts and that He has put His commands deep within us (Jeremiah

31:33). We are obedient to God from the heart, in that we now desire to know God, love God, and obey God. Our new hearts are hearts that make us want to live the righteous lives that God wants us to live. In other words, our new hearts give us a longing for God and a longing to do what is right in His sight. Our new hearts make us want God and make us want to be in His presence.

One of the other amazing things that God has given us for our new lease on life is a clean slate. God has washed our guilty consciences clean. In Christ, we do not have to mope around feeling bad for everything that we ever did. Romans 8:1 says, "There is therefore now no condemnation for those who are in Christ Jesus." We no longer have to try to hide our sins from God, ourselves, or others or try to quiet our condemning consciences with drinking, drugs, overeating, overspending, or any other conscience-quieting, soul-numbing sin. For, as Hebrews 9:14 says that the blood of Christ purifies "...our consciences from sinful deeds so that we can worship the living God. For by the power of the eternal Spirit, Christ offered himself to God as a perfect sacrifice for our sins" (NLT). As you can see from this verse, we have been given a clean conscience so that we do not have to wallow in the mud of godless grief and guilty feelings. Instead, when we remember all the wrong things that we have done we can humbly thank God for "...the blood of Jesus his Son..." Which, "...cleanses us from all sin" (1 John 1:7); we can worship God for the great mercy and grace that He has shown us through His Son Jesus' cross work.

God has given us everything else that we need for a new lease on life through the promises that He made to us in the Bible. Peter tells us that God "... has given us great and precious promises. These are the promises that enable you to share his divine nature and escape the world's corruption caused by human desires" (2 Peter 1:3-4). When Peter says that God has given us great and precious promises, he is talking about the Bible. The Bible is the book of God's promises. It tells us all the ways that we can trust God to make us the holy and blameless children that He wants us to be. We know that God will keep His word; that he will never break any of His promises. For Paul tells us "…all the promises of God find their Yes in him [Christ]. That is why it is through him that we utter our Amen to God for his glory" (2 Corinthians 1:20). Therefore, since God has given us everything that we need for life and godliness through His promises, we do not have to try to be holy people in our own strength. We do not have to try to make ourselves into better people by dieting, reading self-help books, and other self-reforming attempts. Self-reformation is offensive to God because it is the same as saying that Jesus did not need to die for our sins; that He did not need to conquer death to give us new lives. It is offensive to God when we try to make ourselves better in our own strength, because it reveals that we think that what we need is moral crutches for walking in newness of life; not to be raised from the dead in Christ, Jesus. We should not believe the lie that we can make ourselves better without God's free, undeserved grace. God has made us new creatures through our union with Jesus, and He promised to teach us how to live in the glorious freedom of that union. He does this by teaching us how to walk in newness of life; by depending on His Spirit and trusting in His promises.

God has given us all that we could ever need to do His will. He has given us a new heart, a clean slate, His Holy Spirit, and all the promises that we need to live the lives He is calling us to live. Therefore, we should praise God and thank Him for bringing us to know Him. We should think about how amazing God's free, undeserved grace gifts are, thank Him for choosing to give them to us through Jesus' cross work, and ask Him for more grace to believe His Word and trust His Spirit. For God has given us a whole new lease on life. Or, in the Apostle Peter's words, the Lord has given us "…everything we need for living a godly life. We have received all of this by coming to know him, the one who called us to himself by means of his marvelous glory and excellence."

Day 11: The Obedience of Faith

But be doers of the word, and not hearers only, deceiving yourselves. For if anyone is a hearer of the word and not a doer, he is like a man who looks intently at his natural face in a mirror. For he looks at himself and goes away and at once forgets what he was like. But the one who looks into the perfect law, the law of liberty, and perseveres, being no hearer who forgets but a doer who acts, he will be blessed in his doing.

James 1:22-25

Faith is the enabling power of God to believe and to obey God. Everything that goes into saving us from sin has been given to us from God through Jesus Christ. This includes every dimension of our salvation: the payment for our sins, our inheritance, our new lives, our new hearts, our clean consciences, all the saving promises of Scripture, and God even gives us the faith necessary to believe those promises. Faith is an indispensable grace for walking in newness of life, for without faith we cannot even begin to walk in newness of life. Hence the Bible says, "...by grace you have been saved *through faith...*" (Ephesians 2:8). Walking in newness of life is a step by step walk of believing and obeying God's Word.

Faith is a supernatural enabling that God gives to the believer. It is the ability to believe, to have confidence in, and to trust God, so that we confidently obey His word. For our faith in God and our obedience to God are two sides of the same coin. For this reason, the Scripture calls the obedience which results from our faith in God *the obedience of faith* (That makes sense, doesn't it? See Romans 1:5; 16:25-27). You see, true faith in God's Word motivates our obedience to God - we obey Him because we trust Him and love Him (1 John 5:2-3). Obedience to God procures all of the promised blessings of God. This is because obedience is the proof that we truly do believe God. We know that trust in God pleases Him; for Hebrews 11:6 tells us,"...without faith it is impossible to please him, for whoever would draw near to God must believe that he exists and that he rewards those who seek him." **Believing God pleases Him because it magnifies His glory and the greatness of His holiness.** For faith in God shows the world around us that God is real and that His Word is trustworthy.

Second Peter 1:3-4 says, "By his divine power, God has given us everything we need for living a godly life. We have received all of this by coming to know him, the one who called us to himself by means of his marvelous glory and excellence. And because of his glory and excellence, he has given us great and precious promises. These are the promises that enable you to share his divine nature and escape the world's corruption caused by human desires" (NLT). In this verse we are told that through God's promises we become an *active partaker* in the divine nature (i.e.; we become more and more holy in our life's practice), having escaped the corruption of the world. We become a partaker in God's nature by believing the promises of God, and then living in accordance with God's Word *because we believe it.* For, our obedience to God's word is like the hand of faith that reaches out and holds onto the promises of God. Our obedience to God's word is like the legs that walk by faith on the path of God's promises. Obedience to God's word is one way that we receive the gift of His promises. Like an eager child at a birthday party opening her gifts, the child of God receives the precious gifts that her Father bought for her, when she eagerly obeys the commands and precepts of His word.

Saving-faith is the supernatural ability to trust and obey God; thus securing the fulfillment of the promises, which the Lord has made to us in His word. For example, the Christian believes the promise of God that "…if you confess with your mouth that Jesus is Lord and believe in your heart that God raised him from the dead, you will be saved" (Romans 10:9). Therefore she publicly confesses her belief in Christ as Lord in baptism (which is the God ordained practice of one's public confession of faith in Christ - Acts 2:38-39[6]). Her belief in Christ motivates her baptism. In other words, her inward unseen faith in God manifests itself in the outward act of obedience - confession. In confessing our faith in Christ and believing that God raised Him from the dead we are assured of our salvation based on the promise of God that we will be saved from so doing. But, clearly, this does not mean that we are saved as a result of our obedience, rather our obedience is the result of our believing. You see, our belief in God is like the first domino in a row of dominoes: we believe God, so we obey God, which results in receiving the blessings that God promises to all those *who believe Him*. Perhaps you are beginning to understand the Biblical concept of the obedience of faith.

In saying that we are called to walk in the obedience of faith in order to secure the promised blessings of God, we are not saying that we must walk in perfect obedience to God (for no-one living can do that), nor are we saying that we must earn God's blessings to receive them. We have already established the fact that

---

[6] Baptism is the God ordained method of publicly testifying to one's faith in Christ. It is a physical, temporal picture symbolic of a spiritual reality - that the believer has already been united with Christ in His death, burial, and resurrection from the dead (See Romans 6:1-4). Jesus commanded that His followers make a public declaration of faith (testify or confess their faith) in Him through the symbolic act of water baptism. He instituted this policy after His resurrection from the dead, when He commissioned His disciples saying, "All authority in heaven and on earth has been given to me. Go therefore and make disciples of all nations, *baptizing them in the name of the Father and of the Son and of the Holy Spirit*, teaching them to observe all that I have commanded you. And behold, I am with you always, to the end of the age" (Matthew 28:18-20, emphasis mine). Hence, the first time the Gospel was ever preached by the Apostle Peter; he said, "*Repent and be baptized every one of you in the name of Jesus Christ for the forgiveness of your sins...*" (Acts 2:38a. emphasis mine). Also, Peter wrote, "Baptism... ...now saves you, *not as a removal of dirt from the body but as an appeal to God for a good conscience,* through the resurrection of Jesus Christ, who has gone into heaven and is at the right hand of God, with angels, authorities, and powers having been subjected to him." (1 Peter 3:21-22, emphasis mine). Finally, the 1689 London Baptist Confession states, "*Baptism is an ordinance of the New Testament, ordained by Jesus Christ, to be unto the party baptized, a sign of his fellowship with him, in his death and resurrection; of his being engrafted into him, of remission of sins; and of giving up into God, through Jesus Christ, to live and walk in newness of life.*" (The Elders and Brethren of many Congregations of Christians n.d.) This is why I write that baptism is the "...God ordained practice of one's public confession of Christ."

everything that we receive from God we have received freely and undeservedly (by grace). However, we are saying that we receive God's blessings by believing that He really does give blessings to those that trust in Him, and we are saying that real trust in God results in the effort to obey Him.

The Christian life should be characterized by forward motion. Each step in walking in newness of life is a step of faith. We walk by letting our feet land squarely on the solid promises of God's word, and allowing our full weight to rest upon God's faithfulness to keep His word to us who are in Christ. We move forward by walking in an ever increasing obedience to God and to His word. The obedience of faith is exactly that: *it is obedience to God that results from believing God.* It is the hand that reaches out to lay hold of the blessings of God. That is why James says, "…be doers of the word, and not hearers only, deceiving yourselves. For if anyone is a hearer of the word and not a doer, he is like a man who looks intently at his natural face in a mirror. For he looks at himself and goes away and at once forgets what he was like. But the one who looks into the perfect law, the law of liberty, and perseveres, being no hearer who forgets but a doer who acts, he will be blessed in his doing."

Day 12: Sanctification

Since we have these promises, beloved,
let us cleanse ourselves from every defilement of body and spirit,
bringing holiness to completion in the fear of God. 2 Corinthians 7:1

The Bible says, "It is God's will that you should be sanctified..." (1 Thessalonians 4:3, NIV); *to be sanctified is to be made holy.* The process by which one is sanctified is called sanctification. Hence, *sanctification means: process of making or becoming holy, set apart, sanctification, holiness, consecration.* Through the process of sanctification, the believer learns how to live her life on earth in a holy way. She learns how to "...walk in newness of life" (Romans 6:4). You could say that as a believer is sanctified she becomes pure in her life-practices. For it is through the process of sanctification, the Christian becomes increasingly purer in her thoughts, her actions, and her words.

Sanctification is the process by which God conforms the believer to the image (or likeness) of Jesus Christ. God's will is to make all of His children holy as His Son Jesus is holy. Second Corinthians 3:18 says that we are, "...*being transformed into his [Jesus'] image with ever-increasing glory,* which comes from the Lord, who is the Spirit." The same idea is found in the book of Romans where it says, "...For those whom he [God] foreknew *he also predestined to be conformed to the image of his Son,* in order that he might be the firstborn among many brothers. And those whom he predestined he also called, and those whom he called he also justified, and those whom he justified he also glorified." (Romans 8:29-30, Emphasis mine in both verses.) This transforming, sanctifying work of God is a lifelong process for believers. It will have its final fulfillment in glorification when we see Jesus face to face, and we are completely transformed by seeing His glorious presence. The Apostle John said, "...we are God's children now, and what we will be has not yet appeared; but we know that when he appears we shall be like him, because we shall see him as he is. And everyone who thus hopes in him purifies himself as he is pure." (1 John 3:2-3)

As you can see from that last verse, the children of God cooperate with the Lord in His sanctifying work by trying to purify themselves as Jesus is pure; by trying to be holy like Jesus is holy. We purify ourselves by believing and obeying God's word. The Bible says, "God chose you [us]... ...to be saved, through sanctification by the Spirit and belief in the truth..." (2 Thessalonians 2:13). Belief in the truth is belief in God's word. Real belief in the truth activates our obedience to the truth (as we saw in the last reading), and our obedience to God's truth is how God purifies us and makes us holy from the inside out (Philippians 2:12-13).

If we are going to believe, obey, and be purified by God's word we have to know what His word says. To know what God's word says, we must read it, memorize it, ponder it, study it, think about it, talk about it, and (most importantly) live in the truth of it. Romans 12:2 tells the Believer to "...be transformed by the renewal of your mind that by testing you may discern what is the will of God, what is good and acceptable and perfect." Therefore, we must be in the regular habit of reading God's word. The bottom-line is: we need to know God's truth if we are going to be sanctified by it.

Jesus prayed to His Father, "Sanctify them in the truth; your word is truth" (John 17:17). He prayed this way because truth cleanses the human soul from sin. The truth of God's Word sets us free from the lies of Satan, and it also frees us from our bondage to sin and death (John 8:32). Believers are sanctified by, in, and through the truth of God's word. The Word of God is the purifying, sanctifying water of God (Ephesians 5:26); through which Believers are washed and made holy (sanctified).

For this reason, 2 Corinthians 7:1 says, "Since we have these promises, beloved, let us cleanse ourselves from every defilement of body and spirit, bringing holiness to completion in the fear of God." So read you Bible, say your prayers, do the next right thing, and watch God accomplish His sanctifying work through His precious promises; as He produces the holy life of Christ in you, which pleases Him so very much.

Day 13: Sanctifying Discipline

My son, do not make light of the Lord's discipline, and do not lose heart when he rebukes you, because the Lord disciplines the one he loves, and he chastens everyone he accepts as his son. Hebrews 12:5-6

Sanctifying discipline is the training work of God, which results in an increased practical holiness, in the lives of His children. Scripture tells us that the afflictions and hardships of our lives are providentially ordained training sessions intended by God to make us holy. In other words, it is through trials that God most strenuously exercises our faith muscles, and thus most effectively produces the holy character of Jesus in us.

Hebrews 12:11 tells us that, "For the moment, all discipline seems painful rather than pleasant, but later it yields the peaceful fruit of righteousness to those who have been trained by it." The word 'trained' in the preceding verse is a key term in understanding the Biblical concept of sanctifying discipline. It is a word that figuratively means *to train with one's full effort, i.e. with complete physical, emotional force as when working out intensely in a gymnasium; to exercise vigorously, in any way, either the body or the mind.* Sanctifying discipline is about teaching us to believe God's word, training us in godly behavior, and exercising us in the practice of holiness.

Through sanctifying discipline, God especially works on developing our faith. The painful providences in our lives are opportunities to test our faith. Trials reveal where our faith in God needs to be strengthened. Testing makes our faith in God's strengthening grace stronger - by making us aware of our need to experience God's grace. This is why the Apostle Peter says, "In this you rejoice, though now for a little while, if necessary, you have been grieved by various trials, *so that the tested genuineness of your faith... ...may be found to result in praise and glory and honor at the revelation of Jesus Christ.* Though you have not seen him, you love him. Though you do not now see him, you believe in him and rejoice with joy that is inexpressible and filled with glory, obtaining the outcome of your faith, the salvation of your souls." (1 Peter 1: 6-7, Emphasis mine.)

As we walk through our trials with God by believing Him, our faith in Him is rewarded with a deeper holiness of life, a harvest of righteous fruit, perseverance in godliness, and an increase of faith (Hebrews 12:10-14). The pain of our trials make us seek God for a deeper level of faith so that we can believe His Word, obey His Word, and wait for the fulfillment of the promises that He has made to us in His Word. It is the painful sting of trials which motivate us to "…draw near to the throne of grace, that we may receive mercy and find grace to help in time of need" (Hebrews 4:16).

Sanctifying discipline results in a deeper holiness of life because trials burn off the dross of our souls. In other words, trials purify us; they make us turn away from our sin. When we are under stress we tend to want to revert to our sinful coping mechanisms, but the Holy Spirit doesn't let the believer get away with our old sinful coping strategies and ungodly behaviors. He convicts us of the harsh words that we say when we feel stressed, the unkind gestures and faces that we make when we are angry, and the hateful feelings we have when we are thwarted in our plans. He convicts us of our sin, so that we will confess the wrongdoing to God and others and receive God's forgiveness. We become increasingly holy as we repeatedly confess our sins and seek God for His grace to obey His Word. When the trial is over we are kinder, gentler, more humble people; people who are less likely to blame others for our sinful reactions to stress and more likely to exhibit the holy, steadfast character of God (Romans 5:3-5).

Sanctifying discipline results in a harvest of righteous fruit in our lives because trials make us relinquish more and more control of our lives to the Holy Spirit. Trials wear us out and cause us to seek

God for His strength. As the Holy Spirit of God has more control over us, more of His holy fruit is revealed through us: His "...love, joy, peace, patience, kindness, goodness, faithfulness, gentleness, and self-control"(Galatians 5:22-23). It is in this way that God uses our trials to produce a harvest of righteousness in our lives, and He increases our faith in Him.

As we experience deeper levels of God's faithfulness to us in our trials, and we see how He works all things (even really bad things) together for our good; our faith in Him is strengthened. When we experience the merciful compassion of God as He refines us and blesses us as a result of our trials, our gratitude towards Him is increased (James 5:11). As we grow in our faith in God and our gratitude towards God, our understanding of His wisdom in ordaining our trials also grows. As our understanding of God and His wisdom grows, we have an increased ability to trust in God's Word- to rest in His ways, and therefore, we have an increased desire to endure in the obedience of faith. As we endure in our obedience to His Word, we become steadfast in our character. That is: we become more like Christ in our attitudes, words, and actions. Hence, we become what we already are in Christ: the holy, sanctified children of God. That is why the Apostles speak about trials and suffering like this: "...we rejoice in our sufferings, knowing that suffering produces endurance, and endurance produces character, and character produces hope, and hope does not put us to shame, because God's love has been poured into our hearts through the Holy Spirit who has been given to us." (Romans 5:3-5, See also James 1:2-4; 1 Peter 1:6.)

One of the most important things to understand about sanctifying discipline is when God disciplines His children, He is not about punishing us; He is training us. He is forming the righteous character of Christ in our souls. He making us humble and dependent on His grace. In discipline, God is teaching us that we can trust Him, and that He only does what is best for us - because

He loves us. The Lord is not reckless in His administration of discipline with His children, He knows exactly what He is doing by bringing difficulty and hardship into our lives. So, we do not have to kick and scream at the trials of life. Nor, do we have to cower before our Heavenly Father, and beg that our trials would stop. We simply have to trust God and let Him do what He has to do to make us more like Jesus; to make us holy. That is why the Word encourages us, "...do not lose heart when he rebukes you, because the Lord disciplines the one he loves, and he chastens everyone he accepts as his son..."

Day 14: You've Been Warned

See to it that no one fails to obtain the grace of God; that no "root of bitterness" springs up and causes trouble, and by it many become defiled; that no one is sexually immoral or unholy like Esau, who sold his birthright for a single meal. For you know that afterward, when he desired to inherit the blessing, he was rejected, for he found no chance to repent, though he sought it with tears. Hebrews 12: 15-17

Esau was a man who rejected the fatherly love of God because he hated the restraints that God put on His behavior. Esau failed to obtain the grace of God in two ways: selling his birthright and finding no opportunity to repent. Esau sold his relationship with God for a full belly. The Bible tells us that in doing this he"... despised his birthright" (Genesis 25:34). This means that He despised inheriting the promises that God had made to his grandfather Abraham and his father Isaac. By reading the Biblical account, we can see that Esau didn't so much mind the material blessings of God (the wealth and prestige of being heir to the great Patriarchs of Judaism[7]), but he hated the commands for obedience that God required of His people. The Bible tells us that Esau was sexually immoral and unholy. Esau did not want God telling Him how to run his life. He did not want to be told whom he could marry or that he had to forgive the people that had hurt him (Genesis 26:34-35, 27:41, 28:6-9). Esau was the type of guy who wanted to do things his own way. In our day, we would say that Esau was his own man. He did not want to submit to God. And, it

---

[7] I think that Esau wanted the money (his father's wealth), and he wanted the honor due to him as first born (he wanted to be "the man" so to speak). I think this because of the character portrait that Scripture paints of him, and because of his 'babyish but violent' response to his father and his brother- after the blessing was stolen. It is obvious that he had no desire to obey God in that he sold his birthright for a bowl of mush (literally), and because of his choice to have multiple, foreign wives. See Genesis 25:19 to 28:9 to read about this very interesting and instructive family.

is for this reason that the Bible tells us "...he was rejected, for he found no chance to repent, though he sought it with tears" (Hebrews 12:17).

Lest we feel too badly for Esau, those bitter tears that Esau cried were his own doing. Esau forsook God and forsaking God always results in the bitter tears of intense misery and deep anguish of soul. That is one reason that Hebrews 12:15 warns us to, "See to it that no one fails to obtain the grace of God; that no "root of bitterness" springs up and causes trouble, and by it many become defiled..." This is the same reason the Bible says, "Do not be deceived: God is not mocked, for whatever one sows, that will he also reap" (Galatians 6:7). Esau sowed the seeds of rebellion to God: he sold out on God; he was sexually immoral, ungodly, and unholy in his behavior. In time, he reaped the crop of misery that these actions always reap. He sowed bitterness and reaped death; as everyone does that drinks the deadly poison of bitterness (Numbers 5:18-22; 1 Samuel 15:31-33; Hebrews 12:15-17; Revelation 8:11).

When the word says that Esau was not given a chance to repent; it means that Esau had sinned so much that He no longer had any desire for true repentance. Esau's life of rebellion towards God rendered him incapable of repenting from his sin. That is what happens to all people that are given the knowledge of the truth of Christ, but then reject it anyways. The Word warns us, "If they have escaped the corruption of the world by knowing our Lord and Savior Jesus Christ and are again entangled in it and are overcome, they are worse off at the end than they were at the beginning. It would have been better for them not to have known the way of righteousness, than to have known it and then to turn their backs on the sacred command that was passed on to them. Of them the proverbs are true: "A dog returns to its vomit," and, "A sow that is washed returns to her wallowing in the mud" (2 Peter 2:20-22, NIV).

Esau's lack of faith in God caused bitterness to take root in his heart. He did not trust that God was in control and ordering everything in His life for his good so He became embittered when life didn't go his way. He did not believe that God's commands were promises of blessings. He despised the rules that God made because He refused to acknowledge that God was *the boss* of his life. His willful unbelief led him to sow and reap a harvest of bitterness. In the end, his bitterness defiled the ones that he loved most and ruined his relationships (Genesis 26:35).

Esau teaches us that bitter roots grow wild in the soil of willful unbelief. The Bible says "The Lord disciplines those he loves, and he punishes each one he accepts as his child" (Hebrews 12:6, NLT). So when tough times come in our faith we shouldn't jump ship on our faith. Instead, we should choose to believe the promise of Scripture, which says, "...God causes everything to work together for the good of those who love God" (Romans 8:28, NLT). God has more than enough grace for each one of us. He is our Father. He is the provider of all of our needs. Esau learned the hard way that he could not pretend to have a relationship with God. He learned that he could not go to the Word for blessings and, at the same time, ignore God's commandments for holiness. Esau learned that He could not manipulate God with crocodile tears of repentance. Esau learned a lot, and for that reason He can teach us a lot too. The main thing that we can learn from the life of Esau is not to "... Fail to obtain the grace of God..." And, to be sure "...that no "root of bitterness" springs up and causes trouble, and by it many become defiled, that no one is sexually immoral or unholy like Esau, who sold his birthright for a single meal. For you know that afterward, when he desired to inherit the blessing, he was rejected, for he found no chance to repent, though he sought it with tears. ..." So then the moral of the story is this: DON'T BE LIKE ESAU! And, now you've been warned.

Part 2: The Sanctifying Cross

It is for discipline that you have to endure. God is treating you as sons. For what son is there whom his father does not discipline? If you are left without discipline, in which all have participated, then you are illegitimate children and not sons. Besides this, we have had earthly fathers who disciplined us and we respected them. Shall we not much more be subject to the Father of spirits and live? For they disciplined us for a short time as it seemed best to them, but he disciplines us for our good, that we may share his holiness. For the moment all discipline seems painful rather than pleasant, but later it yields the peaceful fruit of righteousness to those who have been trained by it. Therefore lift your drooping hands and strengthen your weak knees, and make straight paths for your feet, so that what is lame may not be put out of joint but rather be healed. Strive for peace with everyone, and for the holiness without which no one will see the Lord
Hebrews 12:7-14

And whoever does not take his cross and follow me is not worthy of me. Whoever finds his life will lose it, and whoever loses his life for my sake will find it. *Matthew 10:38-39*

Then Jesus told his disciples, "If anyone would come after me, let him deny himself and take up his cross and follow me. For whoever would save his life will lose it, but whoever loses his life for my sake will find it. For what will it profit a man if he gains the whole world and forfeits his soul? Or what shall a man give in return for his soul? For the Son of Man is going to come with his angels in the glory of his Father, and then he will repay each person according to what he has done. Truly, I say to you, there are some standing here who will not taste death until they see the Son of Man coming in his kingdom. *Matthew 16:24-28*

And calling the crowd to him with his disciples, he said to them, "If anyone would come after me, let him deny himself and take up his cross and follow me. For whoever would save his life will lose it, but whoever loses his life for my sake and the gospel's will save it. For what does it profit a man to gain the whole world and forfeit his soul? For what can a man give in return for his soul? For whoever is ashamed of me and of my words in this adulterous and sinful generation, of him will the Son of Man also be ashamed when he comes in the glory of his Father with the holy angels.

Mark 8:34-38

And he said to all, "If anyone would come after me, let him deny himself and take up his cross daily and follow me. For whoever would save his life will lose it, but whoever loses his life for my sake will save it. For what does it profit a man if he gains the whole world and loses or forfeits himself? For whoever is ashamed of me and of my words, of him will the Son of Man be ashamed when he comes in his glory and the glory of the Father and of the holy angels.   *Luke 9:23-26*

Anyone comes to me and does not hate his own father and mother and wife and children and brothers and sisters, yes, and even his own life, he cannot be my disciple. Whoever does not bear his own cross and come after me cannot be my disciple... So therefore, any one of you who does not renounce all that he has cannot be my disciple.   *Luke 14:26-33*

Truly, truly, I say to you, unless a grain of wheat falls into the earth and dies, it remains alone; but if it dies, it bears much fruit. Whoever loves his life loses it, and whoever hates his life in this world will keep it for eternal life.   *John 12: 24-:25*

Day 15: Answering the Call to the Cross

And calling the crowd to him with his disciples, he said to them, "If anyone would come after me, let him deny himself and take up his cross and follow me. For whoever would save his life will lose it, but whoever loses his life for my sake and the gospel's will save it. Mark 8:34-35

Cross-less Christianity is Christ-less Christianity, and Christ-less Christianity does not exist. Just like holiness is a non-negotiable for the child of God; cross-bearing is a non-negotiable for all Believers. Jesus saved His people through cross bearing, and, likewise, He sanctifies His people through cross-bearing. Believers are called to take up the cross of Christ by giving up their sin, denying their own selfishness, and living in obedience to God. Cross-bearing will take on different forms at different times in our walk with the Lord, but until glory we will all bear a cross for the sake of sanctification, for the sake of holiness. The call to the cross is a call to submit to the sanctifying work of God, in our lives.

Followers of Christ follow Christ with a cross on their backs and with Golgotha in their sights. Christ calls us to die to ourselves; so that we might truly live to God. He calls us to lose life; so that we can gain that which is truly life. Essentially, the Lord says, "…come and die so that you may go and live." True believers answer Christ's call to the cross by taking up their crosses and embracing the sanctifying discipline of God that makes them holy. They choose a life of submission to God for the sake of holiness. They do what their Lord called them to do; they do what their Lord did. As the Word says, "For to this you have been called, because Christ also suffered for you, leaving you an example, so that you might follow in his steps" (1 Peter 2:21).

Jesus' steps were on the *"Via Dolorosa"*; that is, Jesus walked the *"Road of Sorrows"*, the *"Way of Pain."* He did this in answering His Father's call to the cross. Jesus willingly subjected Himself to the discipline of God for the sake of the sanctification of *our souls*. The Bible says, "For it was fitting that he, for whom and by whom all things exist, in bringing many sons to glory, should make the founder of their salvation perfect through suffering. For He who sanctifies and those who are sanctified all have one source. That is why he is not ashamed to call them brothers" (Hebrews 2:10-11). The Bible also tells us that even though Jesus was perfect, He learned obedience through His suffering (Hebrews 5:8). Jesus took learning obedience to God very seriously, for He suffered to the point of dying on the cross (Philippians 2:5-8). Therefore, we should likewise expect that God will sanctify us and teach us to obey by bringing us through suffering. Like Jesus, we should take learning obedience to God very seriously, as well. We can do this by submitting ourselves to a life of cross-bearing for the sake of becoming holy.

In practical terms, we can answer the call to the cross by giving up our claim on this life- submitting to God through a life of cross-bearing. Answering the call to the cross means owning the truth about our sin, our failures, and our rebellion towards God. And, then, in humility seeking the enabling grace of God to change our attitudes and actions so that they are in conformity to the attitudes and actions of our Lord Jesus Christ. Answering the call to the cross requires that we daily read and obey what we read in the Bible - even when our obedience to God hurts us or costs us something. In other words, answering the call to the cross requires that we consistently choose to do the next right thing and entrust our lives (including the outcome of our obedience) to God's care. Answering the call to the cross means giving up our perceived rights to this life. Answering the call to the cross means leaving our self-centered way of living and embracing a Christ-centered purpose for living. Bottom line: we must answer our Lord's call to the cross. We must intentionally lose our lives so that we might save them. For we know that Jesus said, "If anyone would come after me, let him deny himself and take up his cross and follow me."

Day 16: Embracing the Cross

Shall we not much more be subject to the Father of spirits and live? For they disciplined us for a short time as it seemed best to them, but he disciplines us for our good, that we may share his holiness.
Hebrews 12:9-10

As Christians, we are called upon to *submit* to God as He does His sanctifying work in our lives. *Submission to God means willfully placing ourselves under His authority and intentionally yielding the control of our lives to Him. To submit to God is to recognize and to act upon the truth that we "rank under" God; it is to arrange ourselves under His authority. To submit to God is to gladly obey Him.* Submission and obedience are similar actions, but they are not the same action. Submission is better than obedience. Where obedience is only an act of the will; **submission is an act of the will that comes from the heart.** Anyone can outwardly obey a command if they have to, but only someone that loves and respects the command giver can submit from the heart. Christians submit to God because they love Him and because they trust Him.

Even though Jesus is God (the Son) He submitted to God (the Father) throughout His entire earthly life. Jesus lived as if He ranked under God; He lived like He was only a man - although He was fully God. Jesus put aside all of His rights as God, all of His glory as the Creator of the Universe, all of His power as the Eternal Son of God, and He took upon Himself the humble flesh of humanity. Jesus spent His entire life in willful service to God. Jesus' submission to God was unyielding and from His heart; for our Lord Jesus submitted to God because He loved Him and because He trusted Him. Philippians 2:6-8 tells us that though Jesus was in the form of God, He "...did not count equality with God a thing to be grasped, but emptied himself, by taking the form of a servant, being born in the likeness of men. And being found in human form, he humbled himself by becoming obedient to the point of death, even death on a cross."

Submission to God is focused in its obedience and it is intentional in its faith. Christians must not be aimless in their obedience to God, or vague in their faith in Him. Aimlessness is not a Christ-like quality. Biblically speaking, aimlessness is condemnable; not commendable. We should think about where we have come from, where we are going, and all that we have in Christ; then we will be free to get busy doing God's will for our lives.

Jesus was focused in His obedience and intentional in His faith as He approached the cross. For example, as the time for Jesus' crucifixion drew near, He said, "Now is my soul troubled. And what shall I say? 'Father, save me from this hour'? But for this purpose I have come to this hour" (John 12:27). In another place, we read that "When the days drew near for him [Jesus] to be taken up, he set his face to go to Jerusalem" (Luke 9:51). Just like our Lord *set His face* to be obedient to His Father's will, we should set our faces to be obedient to God's will. We should go where God is calling us to go and we should do what God is calling us to do. In order to do this, we will have to remember that the circumstances of our lives are not happenstance, they are divinely ordained by God for our good and for His glory.

Intentional faith in God is imperative for the Christian life; we must believe that God loves us and that He is at work in our lives; making us holy and transforming us into the image of His Son Jesus. In the same way that Jesus did, we also must choose to believe God and be focused in our obedience to Him, even in the most trying circumstances and the most trying relationships in our lives. Holiness is not a result of the process of osmosis; it is a result of blood, sweat, and tears (Luke 22:39-46; Hebrews 5:7). Therefore, we should be intentional about taking up our crosses and following Jesus - in a life lived in the obedience of faith.

We will be helped in our submission to God (especially during difficult trials) if we recognize that life is short and eternity is long. In other words, if we are to maintain a humble submission to God as He sanctifies us, we must maintain an eternal perspective. We must remind ourselves often that the pain of sanctifying discipline is temporary; the value of the holiness that it produces in us will be everlasting. We must remind ourselves of what Paul said, "…we do not lose heart. Though our outer self is wasting away, our inner self is being renewed day by day. For this light momentary affliction is preparing for us an eternal weight of glory beyond all comparison, as we look not to the things that are seen but to the things that are unseen. For the things that are seen are transient, but the things that are unseen are eternal" (2 Corinthians 4:16-18).

Submission is about willingly and joyfully laying down the control of our lives to God. It is also about acknowledging that everything that we have in life belongs to God first and then to us: our time, our relationships, our family, our money, our pasts, the present, and the future. Submission to God means willfully taking up our crosses (difficulties, trials, and hardships), and embracing a life of humble child-like faith in God. Hebrews 12:12-14 lists the particulars of what submission to God looks like in practical terms. It says, "… lift your drooping hands and strengthen your weak knees, and make straight paths for your feet… Strive for peace with everyone, and for the holiness without which no one will see the Lord." We lift our drooping hands and strengthen our weak knees by praying (Exodus 17:8-13; 1 Timothy 2:1-3,8); we make straight paths for our feet by reading and obeying the word of God (Psalm 27:11, 119:105; Isaiah 26:7); we strive for peace with everyone by learning how to live in loving, joyful fellowship with other believers (Romans 12:10-21; Hebrews 10:24-25); and we strive for holiness by taking up our crosses and following Jesus on the path of submission to the Father's will (See Matthew 10:38-39, 16:24-28; Mark 8:34-38; Luke 9:23-27, 14:25-27; Philippians 2:6-8; 1 Peter 2:21-25; and Hebrews 5:8, 12:1-2).

Jesus submitted to God's will. He willfully laid down His life. The Father did not have to rip anything out of His Son's hands. The Father didn't force Jesus to give it all up; Jesus gave it all because He loved the Father and wanted to do His will. The Lord said, "No one takes it [His life] from me, but I lay it down of my own accord. I have authority to lay it down, and I have authority to take it up again. This charge I have received from my Father" (John 10:18). In the same way, believers have received the charge from God to submit to Him in the process of sanctification. We have been promised that if we subject ourselves to God we will both live and share in His holiness. Therefore, like Jesus, we should also lay down our lives in humble submission to God. We should embrace the cross that He has set before us, knowing that God *"…disciplines us for our good, that we may share his holiness."*

Day 17: Lowliness of Heart

Take my yoke upon you, and learn from me, for I am gentle and lowly in heart, and you will find rest for your souls. Matthew11:29

Humility, lowliness of heart, is an essential quality in submission to God, and an essential quality to receiving the sanctifying grace of God. We can practice ourselves in the art of humility by subjecting our tongues to the control of the Holy Spirit. Subjecting our tongues to the control of the Holy Spirit means not mumbling, grumbling, murmuring, complaining, whining, and pouting every time God brings us through a trial. Those types of behaviors reflect that we do not truly trust God and that we do not truly respect God's authority. Constant complaining about our circumstances communicates to the world around us that we think God is a lousy parent. Part of the sanctifying process is learning how to "Do all things without grumbling or disputing..." (Philippians 2:14).

It is not a small thing in the sight of God to whine, grumble, mumble, murmur, complain, pout, manipulate or to throw verbal temper-tantrums. Furthermore, the Lord equates murmuring against His appointed leadership and mumbling about the circumstances that He has allotted to us with despising Him. In response to these types of behaviors the Lord says, "How long will this wicked community grumble against me? I have heard the complaints of these grumbling Israelites" (Numbers 14:27). In the sixteenth chapter of Numbers, we see just how much God hates rebellious complaining; when a man named Korah led a rebellion of whining and complaining against the Lord and His ordained leadership. The Scripture tells us that in response to Korah's uprising, "...fire came out from the Lord and consumed the 250 men offering the incense..." (v.35). Actually, God was so angry with these men that He told Moses and Aaron "Get away from the midst of this congregation, that I may consume them in a moment."

(v.45). At the end of Numbers 16, we read that, "…those who died in the plague were 14,700, besides those who died in the affair of Korah" (v.49). These incidences show us just how serious it is to God when we use our tongues for murmuring and complaining. The consequences for complaining against the Lord are very severe. Perhaps, this is why James 3:6 says, "The tongue also is a fire, a world of evil among the parts of the body. It corrupts the whole body, sets the whole course of one's life on fire, and is itself set on fire by hell"(NIV).

Also, God hates gossip, slander, and other forms of maligning people. God wants us to love our neighbors - not treat them hatefully by talking about them behind their backs, or, even, insulting them to their faces. When God is using a difficult person to sanctify us, the goal should be to allow that person to be used by God to help make us holy; not to tell them off or to be the one that gets the last dig. We do not want to miss the whole "Sovereignty of God" concept in our sanctifying relationships. Instead, we want to remember that the Lord divinely appointed all the difficult people in our lives, so that we can learn how to be more like Jesus who "When they hurled their insults at him, he did not retaliate; when he suffered, he made no threats. Instead, he entrusted himself to him who judges justly" (1 Peter 2:23, NIV).

Really, the problem with a big mouth is a bad heart. Jesus said, "It is not what goes into the mouth that defiles a person, but what comes out of the mouth; this defiles a person… … What comes out of the mouth proceeds from the heart, and this defiles a person. For out of the heart come evil thoughts, murder, adultery, sexual immorality, theft, false witness, slander" (Matthew 15:11, 18-19). Incessant complaining and chronic whining just reveals a very self-centered, self-absorbed, overly inflated ego. That is not good. It is best to discipline our-selves to stop using our tongues to vent, rage, and manipulate.

Even so, there is no Biblical prohibition to vocalizing our grief in the midst of our trials. **However, God wants us to allow the stress of our trials to lead us into deeper levels of prayer, instead of allowing them to lead us into deeper levels of sin.** When we learn to stop 'venting' with our tongues about life's many (and, often, legitimate) injustices, we put ourselves in the position to learn how to really pray. God has designed us with a need to express our feelings, and with a need to be heard. The appropriate outlet for expressing our stress is prayer; the Lord is the best listener in the whole world (and, by the way, out of this world too). Prayer is the appropriate place for crying out in distress, frustrated tears, and all of the other loud, tearful words of the chastened child of God. The Psalmists teach us this truth repeatedly. They wrote, "In my distress I called to the Lord. And he answered me. Deliver me, O LORD, from lying lips, from a deceitful tongue" (Psalm 120:1-2). And in another place we read, "Out of the depths I cry to you, O Lord! O Lord, hear my voice! Let your ears be attentive to the voice of my pleas for mercy!" (Psalm 130:1-2a). In still another place, we read, "With my voice I cry out to the Lord; with my voice I plead for mercy to the Lord. I pour out my complaint before him; I tell my trouble before him" (Psalm 142:2).

In looking to Jesus, we see the principle of prayerfully crying out to God in times of distress exemplified (Matthew 26:36-47; Luke 6:12, 9:28). Hebrews 5:7 reveals to us that; "In the days of his flesh, Jesus offered up prayers and supplications, with loud cries and tears, to him who was able to save him from death, and he was heard because of his reverence." When Jesus was on the earth, He offered up lots and lots of prayers. Jesus repeatedly went to His Father and expressed His needs, His heart-felt petitions, His desires, and His longings. The Scripture also says that Jesus offered up supplications to God. Supplications in Hebrews 5:7 refers to an ancient custom, in which a suppliant (one who makes supplications) would take an olive branch in his hand as a token that He was 'seeking peace' from a superior. This tells us that Jesus prayed with humility and reverence for God. In our day, we might say that when Jesus prayed He cried His heart out before His Father. He did so with loud cries and tears. This was not considered wrong by God. The Scripture tells us that Jesus "...was heard because of his reverence" (Hebrews 5:7). In another place, we read that Jesus was in such deep emotional distress (in such great agony) in the Garden of Gethsemane that "...he prayed more earnestly, and his sweat became like great drops of blood falling down to the ground" (Luke 22:44). To pray with such deep agony of soul that His sweat became like great drops of blood is nearly incomprehensible, yet this is the example that Christ left us to follow. This is the same Christ who only moments later willfully went to the cross. Yet, Scripture tells us that as He went to the cross, "...he opened not his mouth; like a lamb that is led to the slaughter, and like a sheep that before its shearers is silent, so he opened not his mouth" (Isaiah 53:7).

The example that the Lord set for us to follow shows us that we should allow our difficulties to humble us, and in our humiliation we should learn to seek God for deliverance from our trials. We should not use our tongues to resist God's discipline. We should not use our words to abuse the people whom God is using to sanctify us. Trials (that is, the circumstances, relationships, and other situations of sanctifying discipline in our lives) should be viewed as opportunities to learn to pray - not to grumble against God, or gossip about people. Instead, we should follow Jesus' example; we should allow trials to teach us to pray. Sanctifying trials are opportunities to learn how to trust and reverence God, not disbelieve and disrespect God. Since, Jesus was so humble and reverential to God (although He, Himself, is God), how much greater is our need for humility and reverence before God? And so the Lord bids us, *"Take my yoke... and learn from me, for I am gentle and lowly in heart, and you will find rest for your souls."*

Day 18: A Healing Cross

Come, let us return to the Lord; for he has torn us, that he may heal us;
he has struck us down, and he will bind us up.
After two days he will revive us; on the third day he will raise us up,
that we may live before him. Hosea 6:1-2

In sanctification, God purifies us from every sin-related problem that we have. As we walk in submission to the Lord and His Word, He starts to unravel and undo all the complex soul-destroying results that the sins of the past have had on us. That is; He starts to work through all of the brokenness in our lives that has resulted from sin. He does this because one aspect of holiness is *wholeness*. Just like the Lord took up the saving cross of Calvary in order to make us holy, and we will also take up a sanctifying cross for the sake of becoming holy.

Dealing with the after math of sin is often its own cross to bear. It is not an easy thing to own our part in the destruction that has resulted in our lives; the destruction that has resulted from our own bad decisions. It is even more difficult to own our responsibility in the ruin of the lives of other people that we love (our spouses, parents, children, or friends); but, if we are to be holy, we must do so. We must admit that we have done wrong things that have offended God, hurt ourselves, and injured others. This includes owning our part in the sins of abortion, abandonment, abuse, addiction, adultery, betrayal, dishonesty, divorce, dysfunction, neglect, and other like sins. As the Lord makes us aware of our part in sins like these, we must confess our wrongdoing to God and to others. And, as God allows us to, we must do our best to make amends to those whom we have injured. At times, this will mean exposing our past hidden sins and facing prolonged and, sometimes, severe consequences for them. None the less, in doing this we will be honoring the Lord, who died to pay for the sins that we have committed, and we will be testifying to the world around us that we love God and His truth more than we love ourselves, our reputations, and our sin. And, whatever the consequences of our sin may be, we are assured that the Lord will never leave us or forsake us, and that "There is, therefore, now no condemnation for those who are in Christ Jesus" (Romans 8:1; see also, Hebrews 13:5).

Even more difficult and complex than dealing with the consequences of our own sins for the sake of holiness can be dealing with the consequences of the sins that have been committed against us. It can be soul-wrenching to acknowledge the painful truths of having been abandoned, abused, betrayed, or neglected by the people that we have trusted and loved. Yet, if we are to be holy, we must deal with all the consequences of the sins of the past. Not only the consequences for the sins that we have committed, but we must also deal with the consequences of the sins that were committed against us, as well. For, all of the brokenness in our lives has resulted from sin, but not all of the sins which have resulted in our brokenness were committed by us. Many of our own sin habits, wrong thinking patterns, phobias, disorders, addictions, and our other 'issues' are rooted in the sins that have been committed against us. Therefore, in the process of sanctification (becoming increasingly holy in our practice) the Lord calls us to own the painful truths of our pasts by bearing these sorts of crosses for the sake of emotional wholeness and spiritual holiness.

Often, the things that God calls His children to deal with are the types of things that we would rather forget about. They are the types of things that haunt us and torment us emotionally in our dreams, memories, and broken relationships. These are the types of things that sit at the root of our addictions and sin issues. These are the types of experiences that make us feel powerless and out of control. It is through these types of experiences that we learned that we could not trust anyone - especially a sovereign God, who ordained them. Therefore, it is these types of experiences that God will call us to deal with in the process of sanctification (Romans 6:6; Hebrews 2:15; 2 Peter 2:19b). As we have already seen, our trials are primarily about our faith. Therefore, God will deal with everything and anything that hinders our faith in Him. He will address every incident and action that has rendered us incapable of fully entrusting ourselves to His sovereign control and care.

When the Spirit of God calls us to deal with these types of things, He is calling us to embrace a cross for the sake of emotional healing. The Lord desires that we own the painful truths in our pasts so that we are emotionally free to serve Him in the present. The Lord calls His children to feel the painful emotions which resulted from the trauma of the past; so that we can feel the pleasurable emotions which come from having a right relationship with God in the present and in the future. To answer His call to take up a cross for the sake of emotional healing we will have to acknowledge the sins that were committed against us and learn how to identify those sins and their negative effects with Christ in His cross suffering. In doing this, we will begin to experience the healing power of the cross of Christ. We will experience the powerful truth: "…By his [Christ's] wounds, you have been healed" (1 Peter 2:24; see also Isaiah 53:5).

In calling us to a cross for the sake of emotional healing, God is calling us to be honest with ourselves - even if it hurts. God expects us to acknowledge the deaths that have occurred in our souls as a result of the sins that have been committed against us, and also calls us to accept the losses that we have incurred as a result of those same sins. This is very difficult to do especially if we feel a loyalty to the perpetrators of those sins. However, our willingness to own the truth about wrongdoing is not about condemning the sinner that inflicted the wrong. In reality, it has very little to do with them. It has to do with God, truth, holiness, and our relationship with the Lord. It has to do with emotional wholeness for the sake of spiritual holiness. God promises us that as we acknowledge and accept the truth about our pasts, we will experience His resurrection power in emotional healing. Christ died to set us free from sin, this includes the sins that others have committed against us. He did this so that we can walk in the holy freedom of newness of life in Christ.

As we seek to know, love, and worship God through a life of obedience to Him, He begins to do a miraculous work in our souls. He starts to transform us into the image and likeness of His Son, Jesus. As we embrace the healing cross of Calvary; owning our pasts and acknowledging our need for the healing grace of God; He resurrects our brokenness and our damaged souls in the holy-wholeness of Christ. He makes us holy so that we can wholly serve Him. He does this by making what is crooked in our lives straight and what is lame in our souls strong. That is why Hebrews 12:15-17 says, "Therefore lift your drooping hands and strengthen your weak knees, and make straight paths for your feet, *so that what is lame may not be put out of joint but rather be healed.* Strive for peace with everyone, and for the holiness without which no one will see the Lord" (Emphasis mine.) Therefore, if you have a shameful past - whether by sins of your own doing or the sins that others committed against you - do not be surprised when the Lord calls you to deal with it. Making His children holy from the inside out is the Lord's sanctifying work. Making His children increasingly emotionally whole is part of His sanctifying promise. That is why Hosea bids us, *"Come, let us return to the LORD; for he has torn us, that he may heal us; he has struck us down, and he will bind us up. After two days he will revive us; on the third day he will raise us up, that we may live before him."*

Day 19: Enduring in Faith

And after you have suffered a little while, the God of all grace, who has called you to his eternal glory in Christ, will himself restore, confirm, strengthen, and establish you. 1 Peter 5:10

We must endure in our faith; in our belief and our trust in God. For the Scripture says, "...My righteous one shall live by faith, and if he shrinks back, my soul has no pleasure in Him" (Hebrews 10:38). We must endeavor to believe God and trust that He is always working all things (i.e., all the circumstances, all the relationships, and all the events of our lives) out for our good and His glory, even when this is difficult to do. We must trust God all the time - in the midst of seemingly overwhelming personal weaknesses, broken relationships, and even shameful pasts. We must stand on the solid rock of the promise of God: that He causes "...*all things work together for good, for those who are called according to his purpose...*" (Romans 8:28).

Believing that God will cause all things to work out for our good and His glory can be difficult when those *all things* include abandonment, abortion, abuse, addictions, betrayal, chronic pain, divorce, mental illness, the shame of sexual and physical assault, or the insecurity that results from prolonged emotional abuse. But, regardless of how difficult it may be for us to understand *how* God will overcome our painful realities and transform us through them; the Lord still calls us to believe that He can and that He will do all that He has said He would do for us. Only He expects that we believe in Him. For we know that He has said, "...without faith it is impossible to please him, for whoever would draw near to God must believe that he exists and that he rewards those who seek him" (Hebrews 11:6). Therefore, we must discipline ourselves to trust God and rely on His ability to work out His good will in our lives - no matter how impossible this may seem to be to us. In other words, we must be firm in our faith. For Isaiah 7:9 warns us, "If you are not firm in faith, you will not be firm at all."

Jesus lived and died believing God, and so should we. Jesus lived by the truth that "Man shall not live by bread alone, but by every word that comes from the mouth of God" (Matthew 4:4). For example, it was His belief in the faithfulness of His Father to answer His prayers, that motivated Him to forego the luxury of sleep, in exchange for hours of uninterrupted prayer with God (Luke 6:12). It was also the Lord's faith in God that sustained Him for forty days of fasting and testing in the wilderness (Luke 4:1-2). It was Jesus' trust in God's wisdom to ordain His cross-suffering and His trust in God's power to deliver Him through resurrection, which gave Him the ability to submit to God's will and endure the horrors of Roman crucifixion for His people. Jesus endured all of the afflictions of His earthly life and especially the afflictions that He suffered on the cross by believing in the promises of God.

The promises that Jesus relied upon throughout His life are found in the Old Testament Scriptures. All the books from Genesis to Malachi (the Old Testament) contain promises that God specifically made to the Messiah, who was the long awaited suffering servant of God (Isaiah 52:13- 53:11). For an example in Psalm 16:10 we read, "For you will not abandon my soul to Sheol, or let your holy one see corruption." In this verse, we see that God had promised Jesus He would neither abandon His soul to Sheol; that is, *the grave, hell, or the pit*; nor allow His Son's physical body to decay in the grave after He died physically. It was Jesus' belief in God's ability and willingness to keep this promise (and other promises similar to it) that enabled Him to humble Himself in faith and become "...obedient to the point of death, even death on a cross" (Philippians 2:8).

When Jesus was on the cross He was thinking about God's word. We know this because while on the cross, Jesus quoted from the Scriptures. Eyewitnesses of His crucifixion reported that when

Jesus was being crucified, He cried out with a loud voice "My God, my God, why have you forsaken me?" (Matthew 27:46; Mark 15:34). This quote is taken from Psalm 22:1 where the death, burial, and resurrection of the Christ was foretold. From this, we learn that when the Lord felt most troubled in His Spirit, He held most tightly to His Father's promises. We should be mindful that Jesus' confidence in the faithful fulfillment of the promises of God did not diminish the painful realities of His crucifixion. Jesus really bled, really hurt, and really died on the cross. His trust in God to raise Him from the dead did not belittle His cross-work. Conversely, it magnified it. Christ's reliance on the promises of God throughout His life, and especially on the cross, magnifies the truth that we also can rely on God's Word throughout the duration of our lives, and especially in the midst of our own afflictions. Since the Son of God was enabled to endure the agonies of the cross through His faith in the promises of God; we are assured that **we will be enabled to endure in the obedience of our own faith, in the midst of our lesser trials, by trusting God and by relying on His promises.**

If we truly desire to see God transform the painful realities of our pasts, we must endure in our faith in God. We need to look to Jesus "…the founder and perfecter of our faith, who for the joy that was set before him endured the cross…" (Hebrews 12:2); and be strengthened in our resolve to believe God. We must choose to persevere in our belief in God's power to transform us, regardless of the many complex difficulties in our lives, which have resulted from the sins of the past. We need to rely on God's ability and faithfulness to do all that He has said He would do for us, in us, and through us. God has only asked us to do one thing, and that is to believe Him. If we are going to believe God throughout the trials and afflictions of our lives we must remember the promise of God that "…after you [we] have suffered a little while, the God of all grace, who has called you to his eternal glory in Christ, will himself restore, confirm, strengthen, and establish you."

Day 20: The Danger of Denial

Behold, you delight in truth in the inward being,
and you teach me wisdom in the secret heart. Psalm 51:6

Jesus prayed, "Sanctify them in the truth; your word is truth" (John 17:17). In other words, the Lord asked His Father to use the truth of His Word to set His disciples apart for service to God. He was asking His Father to sanctify His disciples with the truth of the Word of God- so that they could worship God and serve Him in true holiness. God's truth is the key to experiencing the sanctifying work of God. Truth is especially important in experiencing the sanctifying, healing grace of God. Our own painful truths must be acknowledged, nailed to the cross of Christ, and buried with Him in death, so that the effects that they have had on us can be transformed by the truth of God's resurrection power. The Lord sanctifies believers with truth; therefore we must be careful to own truth and stay clear of the many dangers of denial.

Some people think that they do not need to deal with the pain of the past when they become a Christian. They even quote Scripture to justify their opinions; they quote verses like 2 Corinthians 5:17 which says, "Therefore, if anyone is in Christ, he is a new creation. The old has passed away; behold, the new has come." They think that this Scripture and others like it mean that the born-again believer in Christ is not effected by their pasts, because they are new creatures. What these people do not understand is that even though God gave us a new hope, a new Spirit, a new heart, and a new life; He did not give us a new past: He decided to leave our pasts with us for the time being. God did this because He gets more glory by transforming our pasts than erasing them. God transforms our pasts by replacing the terrible truths about our pasts with the redeeming truths of His powerful Word.

In Psalm 51:6 David wrote, "Behold, you delight in truth in the inward being, and you teach me wisdom in the secret heart." This prayer of David teaches us two very important truths about God. It teaches us that God delights in truth, in the inward being of man, and it teaches us that God gives wisdom in the secret heart. This is exactly what God does in sanctification. First, God puts His Spirit of Truth in our inward beings, then He teaches us how to live in the powerful freedom of the Word of Truth, which results in possessing true wisdom, in our secret heart (that is, wisdom in the deepest regions of our souls).

All this to say, we must not deny the truth that God shows us about ourselves or our pasts. This, of course, includes our own painful truths. We must be careful not to live in denial. If we do not acknowledge the bad truths (the sinful realities of our pasts) then we undermine the power of God's redeeming truth in the present. God doesn't let us forget the past, and He doesn't allow us to cop-out of the present. God does not do a mind sweep the second we get saved, nor does He annihilate every person in our lives that has ever caused us to suffer. Instead, He gives us grace to own the messy truths and problem people in our pasts. Then He resurrects the parts of our souls that died as a result of the sins that were committed against us, by the power of the transforming truth of His Word. Therefore, we cannot succumb to the temptation to live in denial about anything in our lives. To do so, would be to forfeit experiencing the resurrection power of God in transforming the pain of our pasts into the blessings of the present.

In reality, denial is nothing more than self-deceit. Denial is a trust disorder. It is an unwillingness to trust God with a painful situation. It is an unwillingness to acknowledge God's Sovereignty in our lives. Denial is a way that we try to circumvent (sidestep) the work of sanctification. Denial is the enemy of truth and the foe of God. Denial is just a fine sounding word for self-deceit and willful ignorance. In other words, denial is lying to ourselves and ignoring the Spirit of Truth.

When we live in denial, we create another world in our minds, a world that does not exist. A world that God chose not to create. It is a way to pretend that the world that does exist - never came to be. Denial is a form of idolatry. It is a way that we worship our own false reality; instead of worshiping the absolute reality of God and His power to create the reality that He has already created. We must be careful to remember that the Lord said, "I form light and create darkness, I make well-being and create calamity, I am the LORD, who does all these things" (Isaiah 45:7). That darkness, which GOD CREATED, includes our own dark pasts. Denial in our lives indicates that we either don't believe God can resurrect our pasts or that we do not believe that God will do what is right by someone that we love (that someone could be ourselves or someone else).

Denial is a judgment that we make; it is a way that we judge God as deficient in His God-ness. We deny reality because we love what we want to be true more than we love the real truth that God has ordained into our lives. If you think about it, denial is a way that people try to be God and try to be the savior of their own little worlds. Denial effectually denies the Sovereign authority of God to be God.

Denial is deeply self-centered at its core. It is self-preserving and self-obsessed. Denial is the mother of every imaginable evil. It is the mother of lies, covering up, excuses, manipulation, and underhandedness. It breeds bitterness, fosters fear, destroys trust, ruins relationships, and in all of these things it enables sin upon sin. Which is so sad; because Jesus Christ died a torturous death to give us grace upon grace (John 1:16). If only people were willing to own their personal truths upon truths.

Believers own truth upon truth because they worship and love the Christ of Truth; whose Father sanctifies them in the truth; through the power of the indwelling Spirit of Truth; by His transforming Word of Truth (John 1:17-18; 16:13; 17:17). Believers know that their messy, painful, sinful truth cost Jesus Christ His life. They know the cost that Jesus Christ paid for the truth. Believers love the truth for they know that the Truth saved their souls from an eternity in hell. They believe the words of Jesus, "...You will know the truth, and the truth will set you free" (John 8:32).

Therefore, we (believers in Christ) are not free to indulge in denial. That is; we do not indulge in the self-deception that sticks its head in the sand, sweeping painful truths under the carpet of satanic lies. Of all the people in all the world, Christians should realize that denial is a form of dishonesty and a practice of willful duplicity. It is a sin that kills all the life that comes into contact with it. Christians must confess any wrongdoing in denial that they are guilty of committing. Through our relationship with Jesus Christ, we have the certain knowledge that God is big enough to handle even the most painful truths that we have to own. We know that our God is powerful enough to transform us with truth and in so doing, teaches us His wisdom, in the deepest regions of our souls. That is why the Believer in Jesus Christ can pray with David, "Behold, you delight in truth in the inward being, and you teach me wisdom in the secret heart."

Day 21: Losing Control

And calling the crowd to him with his disciples, he said to them, "If anyone would come after me, let him deny himself and take up his cross and follow me. For whoever would save his life will lose it, but whoever loses his life for my sake and the gospel's will save it. Mark 8:34-35

Christ said if we were going to become His disciples, we would have to deny ourselves and take up ours crosses by living lives of willful self-denial. Self-denial and cross bearing are non-optional for the true Believer. Thankfully, we have the promise of Christ that by losing our lives we would find ourselves. As Believers we are called to surrender ourselves to the lordship of Jesus Christ - every day of our lives. Giving up our lives for Jesus and the sake of His gospel, requires that we learn how to "...do nothing from selfish ambition or conceit, but in humility count others more significant than ourselves..." It also requires that each one of us is careful to "...look not only to his own interests, but also to the interests of others" (Philippians 2:3-5). If we are going to lose our lives for Christ's sake then we will have to give up our self-centeredness, our self-promoting ways, our heady self-sufficiency, our cut-throat self-preservation, and our constant self-defensiveness.

By way of practical application, we can give up self-centeredness and self-promotion by intentionally drawing attention away from ourselves and towards God. We lose self by losing the abrasive, angry, loud-mouthed, tough girl personality traits, which are so contrary to the gentleness, forbearance, and humility of the Holy Spirit of Christ who dwells with in us. To do this we will need to stop using our words, actions, and clothing to draw attention to ourselves; and instead, use our time, talents, and energy for the benefit of others and the glory of God. We can give up our heady self-sufficient ways by acknowledging our weaknesses, needs, and inadequacies to God, and by humbly asking other people for the help that we need (for as the children of God we should be willing to exhibit the child-like humility that is willing to admit its own helplessness). We can give up our sinful self-preservation by valuing the needs of the people that God has entrusted to our care more than we value the desires of our own flesh. For example, we may forfeit the luxury of wearing expensive clothes or taking vacations so that we can totally give ourselves in service to our families and homes (Titus 2:4-5). Finally, we can give up our constant self-defensiveness by learning to be okay with not having the last word, accepting that we will sometimes be wrongly misunderstood, and by acknowledging the reality that we are not always right.

One problem that we may have with losing our lives for Christ; is that as we do this we can feel like we are losing control. Feeling out of control can feel embarrassing and uncomfortable to us. That is; *it can feel humbling to us*. It is humbling to lose ourselves; it is humbling to feel vulnerable and out of control. And, for those of us who have experienced the emotional traumas of abortion, abandonment, betrayal, divorce, abuse; and/or neglect; feeling vulnerable and out of control can feel very frightening and overwhelming.

However, what we need to realize is that all control (other than self-control) is an illusion. No-body is *in control* but God: because no-body is all-powerful but God. When we lose ourselves for the sake of Christ, and His Gospel (when we give up our selfish ways) we don't make ourselves more vulnerable than before, we don't lose control; we just become aware, *(all be it, sometimes painfully aware)*, that we have never really been in control at all. So, when we feel like we are losing control, we should try to remember that we are not losing control- but, we are really only losing *the illusion of control.*

Losing the illusion of control is the beginning of experiencing Holy Spirit empowered self-control. Self-control is a very freeing grace gift from God. Self-control is the abolitionist that sets us free from the enslavement that we have to our addictions. It is the freedom key that unlocks the door to our new lives in Christ. It breaks our bonds to the fear of man, loosens the chains of insecurity that bind us, and sets us free to walk in the joyful power of fearless submission to God. So, when we start to feel like we are losing control as a result of losing our lives and taking up the cross that the Lord has called us to take up, we can remind ourselves that Jesus said, "If anyone would come after me, let him deny himself and take up his cross and follow me. For whoever would save his life will lose it, but whoever loses his life *for my sake and the gospel's will save it.*"

Day 22: Shameful Truths

But he gives more grace. Therefore it says,
"God opposes the proud, but gives grace to the humble.
James 4:6

The call to the cross is a call to mortify our in identification with Christ in death for the sake of experiencing His resurrecting grace. It is a call to humble ourselves under the mighty hand of God trusting that in due time, He will lift us up (1 Peter 5:6-7). The call to the cross is about trusting God to right all the wrongs that we have endured, and fix all the mistakes which we have made. The call to the cross is a call to own painful and shameful truths about our sin.

Owning truth isn't always easy, but it is always right. Often the truth hurts; that is, it humbles us. Shameful truths expose our weaknesses; they reveal our frailties and vulnerabilities. But, we must own truth, even when it hurts to do so. For God desires truth in the inner man (Psalm 51:6); He saves us by the truth (2 Thessalonians 2:13); we are sanctified by the truth (John 17:17), and set free by the truth (John 8: 32). God is the God of truth (Isaiah 65:16). Christ is ultimate truth (John 14:6), who came in the fullness of truth (John 1:14-17). Not insignificantly, the Lord prayed that we would be sanctified by the truth; that is, He prayed that we would be made holy by the objective truth of God's Word (John 17: 17). Then there is the beautiful and gracious Spirit of Truth - who leads us into all truth (John 15:26; 16:13).

When I use the term "shameful truths" I am writing about the types of truths that result from the sins, which were committed against us, that make us feel uncomfortable and embarrassed to think about and to talk about with others. For example, a shameful truth would be the memory of a parent or another relative crossing the boundary of appropriate behavior with us. Or, it could be a memory of an intoxicated parent berating us in public with cursing and insults. It could also be a memory of some form of sexual assault or physical abuse, which we (or a loved one) endured. It could even be a good memory of a time of intimacy with a spouse who has since abandoned or broken faith with us. When I speak of shameful truths I mean a truth from our lives which makes us feel humiliated or ashamed when we think about it, or when we remember it.

Ephesians 5:12 says, "… it is shameful even to speak of the things that they do in secret." From this verse we can see that the Lord knows that there are some things in this world which are so bad that His people feel ashamed just speaking of them. And, yet, further in this same passage of Scripture we are told that "But when anything is exposed by the light, it becomes visible, for anything that becomes visible is light. Therefore it says, "Awake, O sleeper, and arise from the dead, and Christ will shine on you" (Ephesians 5:13-14). So we see here, that although we feel ashamed or humiliated to talk about certain things, we must expose them by the light of the Gospel if the effects of them are ever to be transformed by the power of the cross. The transforming power of the exposing light of the Gospel of Jesus Christ is a soul-resurrecting power. The Lord has the power to awake us from our sorrow-induced slumber and give us His grace for walking in newness of life. As it says, "Awake, O sleeper, and arise from the dead, and Christ will shine on you."

However, none of this changes the fact that shameful truths feel humiliating to acknowledge. The Lord knows this. He understands the humiliation of being abused, and He understands the contempt of abusers. For Isaiah tells us that "He was despised and rejected by mankind, a man of suffering, and familiar with pain. Like one from whom people hide their faces he was despised, and we held him in low esteem" (Isaiah 53:3, NIV). In all of this, the important thing to remember is that owning shameful truth is a means to receiving grace from God. God rewards the humility, which results from acknowledging shameful truths with His grace. And, when we consider the significance of grace in the Scriptures we are motivated to do whatever we must do to receive it, even if we must suffer some momentary shame in order to receive it.

Humiliation is to make lower in rank, to make low or humble; to reduce to a lower position in one's own eyes or others' eyes. We live in a place and in a time where humiliation and abasement are not valued. But, Biblically speaking, to be or to feel humiliation before God is good. For example, in Isaiah 66:1-2 we read: "Thus says the Lord, "Heaven is my throne, and the earth is my footstool... ....All these things my hand has made, and so all these things came to be, declares the Lord. But this is the one to whom I will look: he who is humble and contrite in spirit and trembles at my word." So you see, it is right to be humiliated sometimes. It is right to be humiliated in response to the holiness of God (Isaiah 6:5). It is right to be humiliated by our own sin (Luke 5:8). It is fitting to be humiliated by our presumptions before God (1 Samuel 15:23). It is right to be humiliated by our foolishness (Luke 14:8-9). To some degree, we do not come to faith in Christ without being humiliated - or at least without being made to feel our own shame and folly. Humiliation that leads to humility is good, even though the humiliation that caused it may have been bad. After all, humility is the quality or state of being humble and God values humbleness of mind, and humbleness of heart. He rewards it with grace.

God promises that He gives grace to the humble, and He also warns that He opposes the proud (1 Peter 5:6). If we are to receive healing grace from God, we will have to own truth that is humbling. The grace that we receive will be in direct proportion to the truth that we have to own. Admitting we were hurt is humbling. Admitting we were embarrassed is humbling. Admitting we are frail is humbling. Admitting we are weak is humbling. Admitting when we are wrong is humbling. Admitting when we were wronged can be humbling too. Acknowledging our dependence on others is humbling. Acknowledging our injury over betrayal is humbling. Acknowledging the brokenness that results from abuse is humbling. Acknowledging shame is humbling. Even crying is humbling (at least, for some people - like me). But, God gives grace to the humble. The more humble we are- the more grace we receive. That is why the Word says, "But he gives more grace. "God opposes the proud, but gives grace to the humble."

Day 23: Scorning the Shame

Fear not; you will no longer live in shame. Don't be afraid; there is no more disgrace for you. You will no longer remember the shame of your youth and the sorrows of widowhood. Isaiah 54:4 NLT

Christ willfully identified with us in our sin and shame, so that we could be set free from the soul destroying effects of sin and shame. One of the greatest of all soul-destroying effects of sin is shame. Shame is that disgraceful awareness of sin or wrongdoing which is accompanied by all sorts of negative feelings of embarrassment. In the same way that wrath is the reaction that God's soul has to sin: shame is the reaction that the human soul has to the awareness of sin. Before there was sin - God was not wrathful and man was not ashamed (Genesis 2: 1-3, 25). However, when sin came, death came, and when death came, man became aware of his profound vulnerability and weakness. That is, when death came man felt a deep sense of shame (Genesis 3: 1-7, 10).

As the image bearers of God, we have a strong, negative emotional reaction of embarrassment to the awareness of sin's presence. We also have a strong, negative and fearful reaction of vulnerability to our awareness of death. These emotional reactions are feelings of shame. Shame, in and of itself, is not all bad. It is an emotion that God designed for our good; it is part of an internal moral alert system. In part, we are enabled to detect sin's presence through the emotion of shame. If sin must be, then shame should be. The Bible warns that God will judge shameless people very severely. The Scripture condemns people who sin brazenly and feel no shame for it. For example, Jeremiah 6: 15 says of the wayward people of Israel, "Are they ashamed of their disgusting actions? Not at all—they do not even know how to blush! Therefore, they will lie among the slaughtered. They will be brought down when I punish them," says the Lord." We can see here that the ability to blush at sin is a very good ability for one to possess.

Shame is a good thing when it leads us to the sorrow that God wants us to experience when we sin. This feeling of shame is good because it leads us away from sin and towards God. Shame can cause us to repent from our sin and turn away from our dangerous habits of rebellion. (See 2 Corinthians 7: 11.) It can prompt us to go to God and confess our sins to Him; knowing that "If we confess our sins, he [God] is faithful and just to forgive us our sins and to cleanse us from all unrighteousness" (1 John 1:9).

However, shame that we feel as a result of another person's sin against us: the shame of rape, abuse, neglect, betrayal, abandonment, or rejection is more complicated to deal with than the shame caused by our own sinful actions. The shame that results from these sins is not our own shame - it belongs to the wrongdoer, but still, we feel it. At times, shame like this can feel inescapable. For, we cannot repent from the action that caused the shame, we cannot confess the sin that caused it as our own sin, and we cannot wash the filth of the sin that caused the shame away.

Sadly, our lives can abound with sinful habits that are rooted in the shame that results from the sins committed against us. People will do anything to avoid the feelings of shame. We will lie, hide, run, ignore, drink, get high, overeat, over-spend, avoid relationships, and even abandon our faith in God (or our attendance at church) in an attempt to avoid the feelings of shame. Adam and Eve went so far as to sew themselves fig-leaf outfits to avoid dealing with shame (Genesis 3:7), and ever since then, humans have come up with countless fig-leaf variations in an attempt to hide themselves from the feelings of shame.

However believers do not have to hide from shame. Jesus knows how to deal with this shame, and He left us an example that we should follow in His steps (1 Peter 2: 21). The shame that we feel as the result of sins committed against us is the same type of shame that Jesus felt when He was on the cross. He was made to endure the ignominy (the public shame) of Roman crucifixion, for the sins of His people. Jesus was publicly stripped of His clothing, nailed to the cross for public execution, and then bled to death on a Roman cross. The Scripture tells us that the torture of the cross was so great that it disfigured Jesus to the point that He was not even recognizable as a human being; as Isaiah 52: 14 tells us, "...His appearance was so disfigured beyond that of any human being, and his form marred beyond human likeness—" (NIV).

Crucifixion was, by intention, a most shameful form of capital punishment. However, the feelings of shame that the Lord felt when He was exposed to the shameful degradation of the cross was, no doubt, secondary to the filthy and horrible shame that Christ felt as "...He himself bore our sins in his body..." (1 Peter 2: 24). The shame of what Jesus was exposed to in the crucifixion reveals to us that Jesus has experienced the depths of our own personal humiliation. The Lord knows the feeling of not being able to make clean that which has been made dirty. As He hung on the cross, our sins clung to His holy soul, and the Father poured out all of the contempt that He felt towards the sin of His people on the Lord Jesus Christ. Jesus willfully endured the extreme shame and degradation of the cross on our behalf, so that we could be forgiven and set free from all the shame-filled consequences of sin. He is the High Priest that identified with us in our shame, and therefore, He is specifically suited for ministering to us in our shame. In Christ, we can be set free the crippling effects of the shame that we feel as a result of the sins of others.

Jesus willfully suffered the shame of the sin of betrayal; so that we could be set free from the sin-induced shame of betrayal (Luke 22: 48). Jesus willfully suffered the shame of the sin of abandonment; so that we could be set free from the sin-induced shame of abandonment (Matthew 26: 56b). Jesus willfully suffered the shame of the sin of being rejected by those who should have loved Him; so that we could be set free from the sin-induced shame of being rejected by those who were supposed to have loved us (John 1: 11). Jesus willfully suffered the shame of the sin of being lied about and falsely accused; so that we could be set free from the sin-induced shame of being lied about and falsely accused (Matthew 26: 60-61). Jesus willfully suffered the shame of the sin of being mocked and ridiculed; so that we could be set free from the sin-induced shame of being mocked and ridiculed (Mark 15:15-20). Jesus willfully suffered the shame of the sin of being abused; so that we could be set free from the sin-induced shame that accompanies having been abused (Matthew 26: 67; 27:27-31; Mark 14:64-65; Luke 23:11-12; and John 19:18). Through the crucifixion, Jesus identified with us in every facet of human sin and suffering; so that in Him we could experience His victory over every aspect of our sin-induced shame.

Jesus won the victory over the sin-induced shame of the cross by *scorning the shame of the cross.* Hebrews 12:2 tells us that Jesus "...endured the cross, *scorning its shame.*" Jesus was victorious over shame. Shame did not cause Him to run and hide. Christ did not allow shame to rule Him, or steal His dignity. Instead, He ruled over the shame of the cross; He stole the power of shame by scorning it. In other words, *Jesus looked with contempt at the shame and humiliation of His cross-suffering.* He looked down on the emotion of shame that he felt while He hung on the cross. He did this in a negative and even in a hostile way. He despised the shame of the unjust trials that led to His death, and thought little of the humiliation of the abuse of His nation and His crucifiers. He viewed the shame of the cross as insignificant and detestable. Jesus treated the shame that He felt on the cross with disregard - He paid no regard to it because, to Jesus, it was of little account. Jesus despised the shame of the cross. *Jesus did this because He knew that the sin of others had no claim on His soul.* Bottom line: Jesus scorned the shame that He felt on the cross, because He knew that it wasn't His shame to own.

In Christ, we can do the same thing. We can *scorn the shame* that we feel as a result of the sins of others. We do not own that shame; we didn't cause it, and we can't fix what did cause it. **However, since we are in Christ now those sins have been put to death with Christ on the cross; they have been washed in His blood - because we (the ones who were sinned against) have been washed in His blood.** The Lord voluntarily identified with us in our sin and shame so that we could be set free from our sin and shame. Now, we only need to believe God. We can own the glorious truth that we have been cleansed from the wrongdoing that was inflicted on us by others. Just like Jesus scorned the shame of the cross because He knew that the sin of others had no claim on His soul, we too can scorn the shame of humiliating abuses that were committed against us. We can do this because (in Christ) that shame no longer has any rightful claim on our souls. And so, the Word says to us, *"Fear not; you will no longer live in shame. Don't be afraid; there is no more disgrace for you. You will no longer remember the shame of your youth and the sorrows of widowhood."* Therefore, let us believe this promise of Scripture, *and let us make every effort to follow in Jesus' footsteps by scorning the shame.*

Day 24: By His Stripes We Are Healed

But he was pierced for our transgressions, he was crushed for our
iniquities; the punishment that brought us peace was on him, and by his
wounds we are healed. Isaiah 53:5-6

The Bible says, "...*sin when it is fully grown brings forth death*" (James
1:15b). Rape, abandonment, abortion, neglect, all forms of abuse,
betrayal, and other similar actions are sin; and they, therefore, lead
to death. First, they lead to the everlasting spiritual death of the
perpetrators who commit these sins (that is, if the perpetrators of
the sins are not atoned for by the shed blood of Christ on the cross).
And, secondly, on varying levels, these sinful actions lead to the
psychological (mental and emotional) deaths of those people who
are victims of them. For this reason, I use the phrases "death-
effects"; "facets of death"; " different dimensions of death" and
other terms when I speak of (or write of) the negative psychological
ramifications of emotionally traumatizing sins. I am using *death-
terms* to describe the different manifestations of psychological
damage that results from soul traumatizing sins, because the Bible
teaches that death is the result of sin. "Death-talk" is better than
"psycho-babble" for describing the results of these sins, because
death-talk more effectively communicates the real problem with
these sins: they lead to death in the human soul; not just
dysfunction in the human heart and head.

When we talk about the emotional ramifications of such soul-
traumatizing sins in terms of death; we are much closer to
understanding the problems which result from them, *from a Biblical
perspective*. A seriously, emotionally-injured Christian is in need of
experiencing the resurrection power of new life in Christ; not the
worldly remedies of self-help books, yoga, endless therapy
sessions, and recovery groups. Emotionally traumatizing violations
are sins against the human soul which result in "soul-death"; they

are not amoral actions for which there are no spiritual remedies. What the emotionally broken Christian needs for healing is the life-resurrecting and soul-redeeming power of God's healing grace; not self-reformation and inner-child-reconciliation.

Rape, abandonment, neglect, all forms of abuse, betrayal, and other similar actions are acts of violence in which the perpetrator destroys certain aspects of the victim's soul irrecoverably. These actions are violations of a person at the most intimate levels of their humanity; they are assaults on the dignity that all humans intrinsically possess as those who are "created in the image of God." The results of these violations naturally end in some form of psychological death. For example, these sins bring about the death of childhood innocence, the death of a general feeling of well-being or safety, and the death of an awareness of personal worth as one who was created in the image of God. Furthermore, there are less obvious "soul-deaths" which result from the aforementioned, emotionally traumatizing sins. There are issues of insecurity, chronic depression, rage, dysfunction, and other equally life-damaging consequences which result from these sins.

Beyond these obvious death-effects, victims of soul traumatizing sins often develop habitual sin-patterns that result in compounding their own emotional brokenness and increasing the deadening effects of the root sins. They are more likely than someone who has not suffered such a severe injury of the soul to fall into the strongholds of bitterness, unforgiveness, addictions, lying, rage, and other soul-destroying sin-patterns. Of course, in saying this, the trauma endured is not an excuse for one's personal pet-sins. As the Lord has said, "The soul who sins shall die. The son shall not suffer for the iniquity of the father, nor the father suffer for the iniquity of the son. The righteousness of the righteous shall be upon himself, and the wickedness of the wicked shall be upon himself" (Ezekiel 18:20). Even so, understanding the location of a sin's root can make weeding one's soul an easier task to perform.

All of our sin issues are dealt with at the cross of Jesus Christ. We are forgiven for our own sin, and we receive healing for the brokenness in our souls which result from the sins of others through our identification with Christ in His death, burial, and resurrection. True forgiveness and real healing come through identification with Christ in His cross-work. God does not reform our old person: He crucifies her, He buries her, and then He resurrects her in the likeness of Christ, so that she can walk in newness of life. That is what Romans 6:3-4 is saying where it says, "…all of us who have been baptized into Christ Jesus were baptized into his death… …We were buried therefore with him by baptism into death, in order that, just as Christ was raised from the dead by the glory of the Father, we too might walk in newness of life."

As a result of the Lord's triumphal victory over death, the power of our sin-patterns and the power of the sins that were committed against us have been defeated. Through our union with Christ on the cross, the manifold and shame-filled consequences of having been abused, abandoned, neglected, divorced, and betrayed have been put to death and buried with Christ in His tomb. Now, through our relationship with God in Christ, we can experience the victorious resurrection life of Christ over all of the different facets of sin-induced death which linger in our souls. For the believer, the death of Christ overcomes all death.

For example, by the power of the cross, God gives us victory over our fear-driven unwillingness to be transparent and gentle in our relationships, and He also gives us grace to give up all of our controlling and manipulative behaviors. Praise God that through our union with Christ, God puts an end to our insecurity, our pouting, and our rage-filled communication. These sinful patterns need no longer rule our emotions or ruin our relationships. Christ overcomes them by the power of His cross.

We can appropriate (i.e., lay hold of, and in practice make our own) the awesome reality of Christ's resurrection by prayerfully acknowledging the sufficiency of Christ's death to atone for our own particular sins, and to heal the unique manifestations of brokenness and death which characterize our lives. In order to do this, we will need to evaluate, *with uncompromised honesty*, the circumstances, the situations, and the relationships which both effected our emotional brokenness, and which are currently being affected by our emotional brokenness. Then we can deal with these truths by bringing them to God on the basis of the finished cross-work of Jesus Christ. We can nail these past events to the cross by systematically and intentionally praying through each painful reality that the Holy Spirit makes us aware of in our lives. We can seek God to administer His healing grace to our souls, and be confident that He will do just that; because Jesus Christ shed His blood on the cross so that believers can walk in the joyful freedom of newness of life in Christ.

Therefore, let us be intentional about contemplating the death-effects that sin has brought about in our lives. Let us consciously and prayerfully name the specific sin-induced deaths which we have experienced. No amount of shame-filled remorse will change what sins were committed against us in the past; nor will any amount of shame-filled remorse change what we did in response to the sins that were committed against us. However, we can be honest with ourselves about the sins that we have committed, and about the sins that were committed against us. By honestly acknowledging the different dimensions of death which have resulted from those sins we can begin to appropriate what Christ has already done for us on the cross. We can begin to partake in the power of His resurrection - and walk in newness of life in Christ. It is by identifying with Christ on the cross - by acknowledging our own soul-deaths - that we will receive healing. Biblical healing results from identifying with Christ in His cross work. That is why Isaiah 53: 5 says; "...He was pierced for our transgressions, he was crushed for our iniquities; the punishment that brought us peace was on him, and *by his wounds we are healed.*"

Day 25: Buried With Christ

And we know that for those who love God all things work together for good, for those who are called according to his purpose. For those whom he foreknew he also predestined to be conformed to the image of his Son, in order that he might be the firstborn among many brothers. And those whom he predestined he also called, and those whom he called he also justified, and those whom he justified he also glorified. Romans 8:28-30

Not every Christian that has ever experienced some form of "soul-death" as the result of someone else's sin needs to embrace the cross for the sake of emotional healing. Some people are instantaneously and miraculously delivered from the death-effects that result from the sins of abuse, neglect, and mistreatment. God delivers some of His people instantly from the death-effects of past sins, and He delivers some of His people progressively from the death-effects of past sins. Either way, God delivers all of His children from the power of sin and death. If you are not presently suffering any negative, painful results from some issue in your past - Praise the Lord! No need to go digging up things that God graciously buried in the tomb of Christ nearly 2,000 years ago.

However, if one's relationship with God is being negatively affected by some event in the past (that is, if we are having a hard time trusting God as a result of some undealt with issue that we have); than we need to deal with those issues. We do this by honestly acknowledging the sins that we have committed, the sins that were committed against us, and the different dimensions of death in our souls that resulted from those sins. In this way, we begin to appropriate what Christ did for us in His cross-death. In like manner, we also need to *accept* the painful realities associated with those sins and the different dimensions of death that occurred in our souls as a result of them. It is in this way that we begin to appropriate what Christ did for us in His burial. Both *acknowledgment* and *acceptance* of the realities of sin and death are necessary parts of experiencing the healing power of God in resurrection. If we want to be raised to walk in newness of life in Christ, we need to come to grips with both the reality and the finality of sin and death.

The question, then, is how does one do that? How does one come to grips with or make peace terms with the sins of devastating betrayals, destructive abuses, or humiliating violations? Or, in other words, how does one "move on"? How does a person "let go and let God"? How does a person accept the actions and consequences of the past, when those actions and consequences are very bad? Well, Biblically speaking, there is only one way to do any of these things, and that way is by *trusting God with them.*

We can accept the past and its deadly consequences by entrusting the past to God. We can come to grips with the death-effects of the sins that were committed against us, by trusting that God sovereignly ordained those sins and their death-effects into our lives - for His own purposes. We can "move-on" by believing and owning the powerful reality that God is sovereign over all of our death. We can "let go and let God" by owning the truth that God is now and always has been in control of our lives.

The Bible is clear that God is sovereign over all of life and all of death (Ezekiel 12:28; Matthew 10:29-30; Acts 4:24; Revelation 6:10). In review, that God is sovereign means that God is unrestricted in power, He has absolute domination, that He has no limitations, and that there are no restraints upon Him. As Christians, we know that God is sovereign. Even so, if we are going to accept the negative consequences that emotionally traumatizing sins can have in our lives, **we are going to need to learn to rest in the sovereignty of God. Hence, the concept of buried with Christ.**

We will need to make a conscious, willful decision to entrust ourselves to God - by trusting that the deaths that resulted from

the sins that were committed against us were ordained into our lives for our good and God's glory. We will need to trust that God was in control of all the events of our lives (even the bad ones) and that He ordered them to the end that through them we would be more gloriously conformed into the image and likeness of His Son, Jesus. In other words, we have to trust that God can and will use all the wrong doing which we have experienced to sanctify us and make us more like the Lord than we would be, had we never suffered any of the effects of sin or death.

Trusting that God orchestrated, or ordained, all the events of our lives - even the bad ones - for our good is not as hard to do as one might think. For, to varying degrees, God may have already used the sins that were committed against us and their ensuing death-effects for our good and His glory. This is the case if God has used any of the sins or death-effects in our lives to cause us to recognize our need for Christ. That is definitely the greatest good that any sin can bring about in any life. There are many other good blessings which result from the bad events in our lives. There is the 'good' of having great confidence in prayer. This 'good' results from having a great need for prayer; such as the need to pray that one would experience the power of the cross in resurrection for the reversal of the death-effects of sin. There is also the 'good' of having a clear understanding of God's word. This particular 'good' results from needing to spend much time in God's word; such a need results from the desire to hear God speak healing, comforting, and corrective truths. There is also the 'good' of having the ability to minister the love of Christ to other people who find themselves in similar circumstances to the ones from which we have come. Even the unique vulnerabilities and weaknesses that we have (as the result of the sins committed against us) are forms of divinely appointed 'good' that God has already worked out for us. For, our weaknesses and our vulnerabilities force us to rely on God's grace (2 Corinthians 12:8-10). By these few examples, we can see how God has already begun to cause the sin and death of the past to work out for our 'good'. The Lord will only continue to do this *good producing* and *God glorifying* work in and through us -more and more - until we are finally and completely transformed by Him in glory.

We can willfully identify with Christ in His cross-death by acknowledging the realities of sin and death. In like manner, we can willfully identify with Christ in His burial by *accepting the realities of sin and death*. We can do this by resting in the sovereignty of God. Ultimately, we can accept the past - no matter what it was like - because we can trust God. We can trust God because we know that He is sovereign over all sin and death. Furthermore, we can trust God because we can see that He has already used the sin and death of our pasts to work out varying amounts of good in our lives. We can trust God because He sent Christ to identify with us in our sin, shame, and brokenness. We can trust God because we know that He loves us. Finally, we can accept our pasts and trust God because "…we know that for those who love God all things work together for good, for those who are called according to his purpose. For those whom he foreknew he also predestined to be conformed to the image of his Son, in order that he might be the firstborn among many brothers. And those whom he predestined He also called, and those whom he called he also justified, and those whom he justified he also glorified."

Day 26: The Hope of Resurrection

...To them God chose to make known how great among the
Gentiles are the riches of the glory of this mystery,
which is Christ in you, the hope of glory. *Colossians 1:27*

The Christian's hope of experiencing the resurrection power of God
in this life is the hope of being increasingly transformed into the
likeness of Jesus Christ, and thus enabled to walk in holiness and
newness of life. Our hope is the hope that we will experience the
power of God in overcoming our sin, our death, and our
brokenness. The hope of experiencing resurrection is not only an
ultimate hope for the believer's future in glorification; it is the daily
realized hope of every believer that is being divinely transformed
through the life long process of sanctification. That is why we have
been learning how to consciously identify with Christ in His cross-
work and burial. We have been hoping to experience the
resurrection power of God in the sanctification of our souls. We
have been hoping that God would miraculously put an end to the
emotional and psychological death-effects in our souls which have
resulted from the soul-traumatizing sins of rape, abandonment,
abuse, neglect, divorce, abortion, and like sins. We have been
hoping to experience soul-resurrection through our identity with
Christ in His sanctifying cross-work. For, **on this side of glory, our
hope of experiencing resurrection is the hope of experiencing
sanctification.**

We have consciously identified our sin and emotional brokenness
with Christ in His cross-death and burial; because we believe the
truth that, "We were buried, therefore, with him by baptism into
death..." We have done this in the hope that "...just as Christ was
raised from the dead by the glory of the Father, we too might walk
in newness of life" (Romans 6:4). Our intentional soul-identification
with   the   cross-death   and   burial   of   Christ   (that   is,   our

acknowledgment and acceptance of the emotionally traumatizing sins from our pasts, and the death that resulted from them) has been motivated by our hope that "...God raises the dead..." (Acts 26:8). We know, from the Scriptures, that God has both the power and willingness to resurrect that which is dead in us through our union with Christ in His death, burial, and resurrection. For this reason, our hope is that God will ultimately cause all of the sins and death of the past, to work out for our good and His glory (Romans 8:28). This hope gives us courage to deal honestly and directly with the sin-induced consequences of death in our lives. In doing this, we rest in the hope of God's faithfulness to us in Christ, knowing that because of it, we are certain to experience His resurrection power for walking in newness of life.

Hope is a joyful anticipation and confidence that a desire that we have will be fulfilled, or will be realized. Our hope in God is our joyful anticipation and confidence that God will fulfill all of the promises that He has made to us in Christ. We rest our salvation on the hope of experiencing the power of God in resurrection. Romans 8:23-24 says it like this, "...we wait eagerly for adoption as sons, the redemption of our bodies. For in this hope we were saved. Now hope that is seen is not hope. For who hopes for what he sees? But if we hope for what we do not see, we wait for it with patience."

Believers hope in the promise that God will ultimately deliver our physical bodies from the death-effects of sin (Sickness, aging, weaknesses, and physical death). So much more, are we not sanctified in the hope that God will deliver our souls from the power, dominion, and practical control of sin in our daily life experience? Indeed, we joyfully anticipate the day that God will instantly transform our sin-sick and death-sentenced bodies into sin-free, immortal, imperishable, and incorruptible bodies; bodies that will be perfectly suited for eternal life in the presence of God (1 Corinthians 15:49-55, See the whole chapter, and esp. v.49; 1 John 3: 1-3).

Likewise, we joyfully anticipate and experience the progressive transformation of our souls into conformity with the person of Christ, as God daily does His sanctifying work in our lives, by the power of Christ's resurrection life at work within us (Ephesians 1: 17-21; Philippians 2:13; 2 Corinthians 3:18, 4:7). We live the entire Christian life in a moment by moment hopefulness of experiencing the resurrection power of God for walking in holiness and newness of life. We rest in the hope that God will fulfill His promises to make us holy. We know that our hope in God "...does not put us to shame, because God's love has been poured into our hearts through the Holy Spirit who has been given to us" (Romans 5:5). Therefore, we heed the admonition of 2 Corinthians 7:1 which says, "Since we have these promises, beloved, let us cleanse ourselves from every defilement of body and spirit, bringing holiness to completion in the fear of God."

The hope of experiencing resurrection emboldens our pursuit of holiness, for the Word of God teaches that we will all give and account to God and that without holiness, no one will see the Lord (Hebrews 4:13, 9:27, 12:14). Therefore, we pursue holiness in the hope of experiencing resurrection. And, in a sense, each conquest of holiness in our lives is an experience of soul-resurrection. It is an experience of God resurrecting our souls in the holy likeness of Jesus Christ, our Lord. The Apostle Paul wrote, "Though our outer self is wasting away, our inner self is being renewed day by day" (2 Corinthians 4:16). That daily inner renewal which Paul wrote about is a soul-resurrection of sorts. It is a transformation of our souls in the likeness of Christ. Through the power of God in resurrection, "...the new self... ...is being renewed in knowledge after the image of its creator" (Colossians 3:10). And, each victory of holiness in our lives is a foretaste of our coming experience of total transformation at the physical resurrection and redemption of our bodies.

When it comes to the hope of experiencing resurrection, we are hoping to experience the power of God working through our union with Christ. For the Lord said, "I am the resurrection and the life. Whoever believes in me, though he die, yet shall he live" (John 11:25). In the believer's experience of resurrection, God is the acting agent; the giver of all new life in Christ (Acts 26:8; Romans 1:4, 6:4; 2 Corinthians 1:9; 5:16-19; Titus 3:4-7). Therefore, our hope to experience resurrection is a hope to experience the power of God in our lives. For, only God can take something very broken in our souls and heal us; only God can take something that dies in our souls and restore life to us. God is the one who takes the decaying corpses of our pasts and by the His soul-resurrecting power-transforms them (that is, transforms who we have become as a result of our pasts) into spiritually living, Holy Spirit controlled new creatures in Christ. By the power of the resurrection of Jesus Christ, God makes us new creatures (despite whatever sin and death-effects have characterized our lives). As 2 Corinthians 5:16-17 says, "From now on, therefore, we regard no one according to the flesh. Even though we once regarded Christ according to the flesh, we regard him thus no longer. Therefore, if anyone is in Christ, he is a new creation. The old has passed away; behold, the new has come." God crucified our sin-infested, death-encrusted souls with Christ on the cross, buried all of our sin and death-effects in Christ's tomb, and it is God who supernaturally resurrects our souls in the likeness of His Son, Jesus Christ. As God does this, as He sanctifies us, we experience the resurrecting power of God on *this side of glory*. In this way, we experience God in the here and now of our lives.

But what is meant by saying that God resurrects our souls in the likeness of His Son, Jesus Christ? Well, obviously, this does not mean that we become Jesus. It does not mean that God takes a super-sized divine eraser and erases our pasts. It does not mean that we feel happy all the time. And, it does not mean that everything in our lives instantly (or maybe even ever) works out the way that we think that our lives should work out. It means that we become increasingly like Jesus in our inner-person, in our souls. It means that we become increasingly holy, sanctified, and consecrated to God for fruitful service in our daily lives. It means that we experience soul-resurrection as the power of God works in and through us manifesting the life of His Son and transforming us into His holy children.

Thus, we consciously identify with Christ in His death and burial in the hope of experiencing identity with Him in His resurrection life. We appropriate the power of the cross of Christ for emotional healing in the hope (in the joyful anticipation) of experiencing the power of God in resurrection as He sets us free from the power of soul-destroying sins. We identify with Christ in His death and suffering in the hope that God will sanctify us, by transforming us into the likeness of Christ. We identify with Christ in His cross-work because by dying to the sin that has held us in its grip, we are set free to serve God. As we appropriate the death of Christ, we are sanctified and we are prepared to inherit eternal life. That is why Romans 6:22 says, "...now that you have been set free from sin and have become slaves of God, the fruit you get leads to sanctification and its end, eternal life."

Ultimately, we are motivated to identify with Christ in death and burial by our hope of experiencing an identification with Him in His resurrection. And, on this side of glory, the hope of experiencing resurrection is the hope of experiencing a deeper level of sanctification (holiness, purity, and consecration for fruitful service to God). Our hope of experiencing resurrection is the hope of experiencing greater transformation into the image and likeness of our Savior, Jesus. In other words, in this life, our hope of experiencing resurrection is the hope of practically experiencing the glorious riches of this mystery: "...Christ in you [us], the hope of glory."

Day 27: Set Free From Sin

But now that you have been set free from sin and have become slaves of
God, the fruit you get leads to sanctification and its end, eternal life.
Romans 6:22

Jesus said, "If anyone would come after me, let him deny himself and take up his cross daily and follow me" (Luke 9:23). Christ calls His followers to die to themselves to the end that we experience the power of God in resurrection and are thus enabled to walk in newness of life in Christ. We experience the power of God in resurrection as we die to the death-effects of the sins which have dominated our lives and begin to walk in newness of life, through the resurrecting power of His indwelling Spirit. By letting go of our past relationship with sin and death through the power of the cross; we are set free to walk in newness of life through the resurrection of Christ.

In practical terms experiencing the resurrection power of God for walking in newness of life, means that God sets us free from the entanglements and power of sin in our daily lives. In practical terms, this means that God breaks the bonds of the past which held us as slaves to our former lusts. It means through our faith in Christ; we truly can say "No!" to sin and death, and say "Yes!" to God by saying, "Yes!" to holy living. Because of the resurrection, we no longer have to indulge our base desires; quiet our condemning consciences, or soothe our wounded souls with drugs, sex, co-dependent relationships, over-eating, over-spending, or by practicing any other form of sin. Instead, by God's resurrecting, transforming grace, we can leave our sinful pasts buried with Christ, and in this very moment we can live holy lives. For in Christ and through the power of His resurrection - we are sanctified in our thinking, speaking, and behavior.

Through the resurrection life of Christ, God sets us free from our sinful rage-filled, self-justifying, and lustful thoughts; by enabling us to replace them with peace loving, God exalting, and soul purifying thoughts. For example, when a shame-filled, soul-destroying memory comes to mind, one which leads to irrational thoughts of revenge or fantasies of 'getting even' with people who have sinned against us; God enables us to replace those base thoughts with Godly prayers. God frees us to "...Love your [our] enemies and pray for those who persecute you [us]..." (Matthew 5:44). Now, instead of indulging our sinful thoughts of revenge, we are free in Christ, to pray that God will use the sins that our enemies committed against us, to see (with their spiritual eyes) their need for repentance and faith in Christ. In other words, because of the vindicating power of the resurrection, we are set free to forgive[8] and pray for the salvation of the people who have hurt us - instead of day-dreaming about getting even with them. We can also seek God for the resurrection grace not to dwell on the trespasses that

---

[8] A word on forgiveness: The Lord requires that we forgive our enemies; that we forgive the people that have injured us (Matthew 6:14-15; Colossians 3:13). We must forgive as we have been forgiven, that is what we (Christians) pray - that is what we (Christians) believe (Luke 11:4). If we know Christ, and have experienced His forgiveness - extended to us - through the cross, extending forgiveness to others is not an impossibility. Rather it is a divinely enabled act of our wills. After Jesus' resurrection from the dead, He appeared to His disciples, spoke words of peace to them, commissioned them to His service, breathed on them, and said, "Receive the Holy Spirit. If you forgive the sins of any, they are forgiven them; if you withhold forgiveness from any, it is withheld" (John 20:23, context verses 19-23). From this we can see that all true Disciples of Christ are *divinely enabled* to extend forgiveness to all people, at all times. It is important to understand that forgiveness does not always mean reconciliation within our human relationships; but it does always involve a true desire, on our part, to see the offending party (those that have hurt us) restored to a right relationship with God, and if possible with us. Bottom line: We must forgive the people that have hurt us: it is the way of the cross, it is the way of Christ. We can forgive anybody and everybody because of the cross-work of Christ. We can forgive because of the resurrection power of God at work in our souls. And, ultimately, we can forgive because we know and understand that God is sovereign and that He has ordained all of the evils of this world and this age to ultimately work for His glory and our good: Remember Romans 8:28-30 and Ephesians 1:3-6, 11-12. If you are struggling with forgiving someone who has hurt you, I highly recommend the following resource by June Hunt: Hunt, June. 2007. *How to Forgive...When You Don't Feel Like It*. Eugene, Oregon. Harvest House Publishers.

others have committed against us, knowing that (somehow) God will use all of those trespasses for our good and His glory.

Another example of how through the power of Christ's resurrection, we can replace bad thoughts with God-glorifying thoughts, is in the realm of lustful thinking. When a lustful thought of sensual immorality comes to our minds, one that has its roots in the cesspools of a sexual relationship outside of a Biblically sanctioned marriage; we can turn away from our inordinate desires by singing praises to God and meditating on the holiness, purity, and splendor of Jesus Christ. Furthermore, in Christ we put away watching immoral television and reading the smut, which feeds lustful thinking; and instead spend what little free time that we have, meditating on "...whatever is true, whatever is honorable, whatever is just, whatever is pure, whatever is lovely, whatever is commendable... .....Any excellence, ...Anything is worthy of praise" (Philippians 4:8).Through the resurrection life of Christ we obey the admonition of Scripture, "Do not be conformed to this world, but be transformed by the renewal of your mind, that by testing you may discern what is the will of God, what is good and acceptable and perfect" (Romans 12:2).

Through the power of the resurrection of Christ, we are also set free from our former patterns of communication which are characterized by deceit, manipulation, and self-aggrandizing speech. Instead of speaking in those ways, we are free to speak kind, up-building, and gentle words (even when we have to speak with irritating and frustrating people). For the same reason, we can be respectful to all of the people that are in authority over us; regardless of how worthy they are of our respect. We know the truth that "...there is no authority except from God, and those that exist have been instituted by God" (Romans 13:1), and so we can speak respectfully to and about all the God-ordained authority figures in our lives. We can do this because we know that since God is sovereign over even the resurrection of the dead, He is also sovereign over all things in life- including the various authority figures with whom we must interact.

Nor do we any longer have to be like the insecure fool who takes "...no pleasure in understanding, but only in expressing his opinion" (Proverbs 18:2). In Christ we are set free from the sin-induced insecurity that motivates the proud and boastful know-it-all type speech, which so often characterizes the women of the world. Because of the resurrection power of God in Christ, we have the knowledge that we are safe in God's care, that God is in control of everything; so we do not need to always be "blabbing our heads off"; acting like we know everything that is to be known about life. (Please, excuse my use of a third-grader-expression, it just seems to perfectly describe what I am trying to explain.)

Furthermore, through the power of Christ's resurrection, we are also set free from the using our tongues as "weapons of mass-destruction". That is, we no longer have to use our mouths to spew-out blasphemous and venomous insults to every person that even slightly crosses us. Instead, we can obey the command of Scripture to "Bless those who persecute you [us]; bless and do not curse them" (Romans 12:14).We can do this because we know that the Lord has said, "Vengeance is mine, I will repay" (Romans 12:19). And, since God is God-enough to resurrect the dead, we can trust that He is also God-enough to "...repay each person according to what they have done" (Romans 2:6). The Bottom line is this: by experiencing the power of God in resurrection we know that we are safe in the care of God; so we no longer have to use our words to try to keep ourselves safe. Instead, we are able to live in the glorious and life-giving truth that "In returning and rest you [we] shall be saved; in quietness and in trust shall be your [our] strength" (Isaiah 30:15).

Finally, through the power of the resurrection life of Christ, we are set free from our sinful, self-serving life-styles, and given the freedom to live lives for the service and glory of God. Now, through our relationship with God in Christ, we can practice the same humility of our Lord who "...though he was in the form of God, did not count equality with God a thing to be grasped, but emptied himself, by taking the form of a servant..."(Philippians 2: 5-7). In humility, we can "...count others more significant than yourselves [ourselves]" by looking "...not only to his [our] own interests, but also to the interests of others" (Philippians 2: 3-4). In other words, we do not have to spend the rest of our lives proving that we are important; striving to manipulate every situation in which we find ourselves to our own benefit; or using people trying to accomplish our ends in life. Instead, because of the power of the resurrection, we can pray "Your kingdom come, you're will be done, on earth as it is in heaven" (Matthew 6:10), and then we can live as if we meant that prayer from our hearts by submitting to one another out of love (Ephesians 5:21).

In the power of Christ's resurrection, we "...live for the rest of the time in the flesh no longer for human passions but for the will of God" (1 Peter 4:2); being "...careful to devote themselves [ourselves] to good works" (Titus 3:8). Through the power of the resurrection life of Christ, we have been set free to "...clothe yourselves [ourselves]... With the beauty that comes from within, the unfading beauty of a gentle and quiet spirit, which is so precious to God." (1 Peter 3:4). And this is true, regardless of what kind of background we come from, our particular given personalities, what sins were formerly committed against us, or what sins we formerly committed. You see, when we experience the power of God in resurrection we are enabled by God to walk in newness of life.

These are just a few examples of being set free to walk in newness of life through the resurrection power of Christ. These "real life" examples flesh-out what it means to live life in the resurrection power of Christ, and to walk in newness of life in Him. You see, through the resurrection life of Christ, we are set-free from everything that we hate, set free from everything that is killing us and killing the people that we love. And, we are set free to enjoy everything that we love; everything that makes us holy, and everything that gives us life. That is what the Word means where it says, "...you [we] have been set free from sin and have become slaves of God, the fruit you [we] get leads to sanctification and its end, eternal life"

Day 28 Walking in Newness of Life

What shall we say then? Are we to continue in sin that grace may abound? By no means! How can we who died to sin still live in it? Do you not know that all of us who have been baptized into Christ Jesus were baptized into his death? We were buried therefore with him by baptism into death, in order that, just as Christ was raised from the dead by the glory of the Father, we too might walk in newness of life.
Romans 6:1-4

The point of this devotional has been learning (in practical terms) how to walk in newness of life. I have sought to show the reader how, through an intentional identification with Jesus in His death and burial, we can experience the power of God in resurrection for walking in newness of life. I have sought to share how the believing woman can learn to view each affliction, difficult relationship, and painful circumstance in her life as a divinely appointed opportunity to take up her cross and follow Jesus, to the end that she would experience the soul-resurrecting sanctifying-grace of God. In short, I have written this devotional in the hope of communicating a practical Christ-centered and cross-embracing way of living. My desire in doing this has been that we might see *the practical ramifications* of our union with Christ and understand (a little more experientially) the sovereign power and great love of God at work in our lives to cause everything (including the bad things in our lives) to ultimately work together for our good and His glory.

Really, we have simply spent 28 days looking at our lives through the lens of gospel truth. We have been trying to unfold *the practical nature* of what it means that we who are in Christ have been crucified with Christ and, therefore, we no longer live, but, instead, it is Christ who lives in us. We have reviewed the fundamentals of living the lives God has given us by faith in the Son of God, who loved us and gave himself for us (See Galatians 2:20). We have done this by focusing on our identification with Christ in His death and burial; focusing on how we can take up our God ordained crosses and follow our Lord in a life of faith-filled submission and obedience to His will. I have focused on identification with Christ in His cross-work and burial because for me this was the gateway to experiencing the resurrection power of God for walking in newness of life.

Instead of focusing on how to appropriate the resurrection and new life in Christ, our focus has been on understanding how to *appropriate the cross in real life* by obeying Christ's command to take up our crosses and follow Him in a life of self-denial. It is my understanding that both experiencing the resurrection power of God and experiencing victory in walking in newness of life in Christ are by the super-natural working of God. Therefore, these meditations have been geared towards guiding the reader towards understanding the practical ways that we can embrace the cross of Christ. For by embracing the cross, I believe that we demonstrate our faith in God's willingness to bestow His children with the super-natural resurrection grace, which is necessary for walking in newness of life. In the same way, (i.e., by embracing our providentially ordained crosses), we also properly prepare our souls to experience the true resurrection power of God for walking in newness of life (Romans 6:1-4)

We began our journey in *Part 1 The Sanctified* by reviewing the basics of Christianity. In week one of our study, we learned that walking in newness of life means understanding that God is holy, and for this reason we can trust Him. We also learned that the Word of God is a light unto our paths and a lamp for our feet as we walk in newness of life. We received the warning that if we are to walk in newness of life we must stay off the treacherous paths of entangling sin. We also saw that we should thank God for the merciful roadblocks that keep us off the roads that lead to hell. Most importantly, we learned that we can only walk in newness of life through the cross of Christ and by the power of God. Lastly, in week one, we learned that walking in newness of life means walking in the life long practice of confessing and repenting of our remaining sinful habits and practices.

In week two of our study, we moved beyond the basics and began to look at some of the particular blessings of the Christian life. Most importantly we learned (in at least a basic way) what it means that we have union with Christ. We also learned that as the beloved children of God, we have been given an inheritance of grace. We learned that because of the cross-work of Jesus Christ we have a whole new lease on life; that is, we have been given a new heart and a clean conscience so that we can serve God. In week two, we also learned that God has equipped Christians with everything that they need so that they can walk in the obedience of faith. After this, we considered the purpose and process of sanctifying discipline. That is, we learned that God sanctifies His children and trains them so that they can be holy. Last of all in week two, *we were warned:* we do not want to play games with God; that we must not be like Esau.

In *Part Two: The Sanctifying Cross* looked at the process of sanctification (becoming holy) in the light of the Lord's call to the cross. In week three, we began to consider what it means that Christ calls us to the cross. We saw that we must embrace the cross, which the Lord calls us to embrace in submission to God, and for the sake of personal holiness. We learned that submission to God includes taming our tongues and learning to pray to God in times of distress. During week three, we also saw that we must endure in our faith in the midst of trials, embrace the truth that the Lord shows us, and (at all costs) avoid the dangers of denial. Finally, in week three, we saw that sometimes God calls us to embrace the cross for the sake of emotional healing, and that this may mean that we must embrace shameful truths in order to receive God's healing and redeeming grace.

In our last week of devotions, we learned that we must give up our illusions of control so that we can receive the gracious gift of self-control. We also learned that if we want to experience the freedom of new life in Christ we will we need to scorn the shame of the sins that were committed against us in the past. In the final days of our study, we saw that *through identification with Christ in His death we can acknowledge painful truth; and through identification with Him in His burial we can also accept painful truth.* We saw that in so doing, we will receive the supernatural healing grace of God in our souls. That is, we will experience the power of God in resurrection. Finally, we learned that it is through our union with Christ in His resurrection that we are set free from sin, and enabled to walk in the glorious newness of life in Christ.

Habits of holiness and the power for walking in newness of life are the fruit of the indwelling presence of Christ in the believer's life. These fruitful manifestations of the life of Christ come to life in our souls only after the seeds of our own self-sufficiency, self-importance, and self-preservation die in the rich and fertile, soil of persevering faith. Often, it is only after these seeds of death are watered by the terrible storms of life that the believer can begin to see that every painful providence has been ordained by God to prepare her heart for His Kingdom rule, and to prune her soul in order that He can reap a fruitful harvest of righteous fruit for her good and His glory. It is only after our illusions of autonomy have died on the cross with Christ and have been buried with Him in the empty tomb that we understand that walking in newness of life means walking in the soul-resurrecting and life redeeming power of God. For, it is only after we die to ourselves that we can begin to experience the power of God in resurrection. It is only after we bury our own concepts of what is good in us and what is worthy of keeping in our pasts that we can begin to see the wisdom of God in ordaining specific afflictions into our lives. Only then, can we begin to see with our spiritual eyes, how it is that God is ultimately and sovereignly using all things in our lives to conform us into the holy image of His Son and our Lord, Jesus Christ (Romans 8:28-29).

There is so much more that could be said about walking in newness of life. In this series of short essays we have only begun to consider 28 "baby steps" in walking in newness of life. For, we have focused only on wholeness in holiness, which is a small part of the Christian walk. We have considered understanding how we can fellowship with Christ in His sufferings - to the end that we can begin to experience the power of our union with Him in resurrection and newness of life. But this does not even scratch the surface of walking in newness of life. For the new life that we have been given in Christ is an eternal life, and therefore entails an everlasting journey for all those who are called to take it.

In Jesus' high priestly prayer, He said, "And this is eternal life, that they know you the only true God, and Jesus Christ whom you have sent" (John 17:3). Knowing the only true God and knowing Jesus whom God sent into the world is the eternal life in which we have just begun to walk. Each step that we have taken on the cross-walk has been intended to lead us into a more and more intimate, experiential knowledge of God - and, each step which we have taken towards identifying with Christ in His death has been a step in the obedience of faith. That is, each step that we have taken in walking in newness of life has been taken because we believe in God and we believe that through our union with Christ we will experience His resurrection power. Along the same lines of thinking the Apostle Paul wrote, "I count everything as loss because of the surpassing worth of knowing Christ Jesus my Lord. For his sake I have suffered the loss of all things and count them as rubbish, in order that I may gain Christ and be found in him, not having a righteousness of my own that comes from the law, but that which comes through faith in Christ, the righteousness from God that depends on faith—that I may know him and the power of his resurrection, and may share his sufferings, becoming like him in his death, that by any means possible I may attain the resurrection from the dead" (Philippians 3: 8-11).

Personally, I cannot imagine a way that we could possess a more intimate knowledge of God than having Him inside of us in the person of the Holy Spirit, manifesting His resurrection power through our physical, mental, and emotional capacities; literally changing us from the inside out, and thus enabling us to walk in newness of life in Christ. Yet, astonishingly, this is exactly what has been happening in us since the moment that God saved us. God has been making us more and more holy, conforming us into the image of His Son. He has been forgiving sin. He has been at work healing that which is lame in us. He has begun to unravel our twisted sinful thinking and untangle all the shame filled knots in our souls. God has only begun to resurrect that which is dead in us; teaching us how to walk in the glorious newness of life that He has so graciously given us in Christ. Since the moment that we passed from death to life, God Himself has been at work in our souls producing all of the necessary graces that we have needed for walking in newness of life- through our union with Christ. Every step of faith that we have taken, every act of obedience which we have completed, every willingness and inclination towards God's will has been a fulfillment of both the exhortation and the promise of Philippians 2:12-13: "Therefore, my beloved, as you have always obeyed, so now, not only as in my presence but much more in my absence, work out your own salvation with fear and trembling, for it is God who works in you, both to will and to work for his good pleasure." *Living in the reality of this verse is walking in newness of life.*

In John 11: 25-26 the Lord tells Martha the most powerful truth that has been told to anyone in this world. He said to her, "I am the resurrection and the life. Whoever believes in me, though he die, yet shall he live, and everyone who lives and believes in me shall never die." After this, He asked her an important question, a question that we must answer, as well. He asked her, "Do you believe this?" She rightly responded, "Yes, Lord; I believe that you are the Christ, the Son of God, who is coming into the world." And so, the end of the matter is this: for those of us that agree with Martha, and affirm that Jesus Christ is the Son of God sent into the world to claim a people of His own through His blood shedding death on the cross, His burial, and His resurrection; we have the certain promise of God that "…just as Christ was raised from the dead by the glory of the Father, we too might walk in newness of life." Amen. Even so, come Lord Jesus.

What shall we say then? Are we to continue in sin that grace may abound? By no means! How can we who died to sin still live in it? Do you not know that all of us who have been baptized into Christ Jesus were baptized into his death? We were buried therefore with him by baptism into death, in order that, just as Christ was raised from the dead by the glory of the Father, we too might walk in newness of life.
Romans 6:1-4

Glossary of Terms

Appropriate lay hold of, or make one's own.

Atonement full payment for sin.

Baptize dip, submerge.

Confession giving full consent to, being in out-and-out agreement with, admitting wrongdoing, or an acknowledgement of debts owed.

Exhort strongly encourage, urge.

Fallible capable of making mistakes; subject to error.

Glory of God The overflowing radiance and the brilliance of the holiness of God (i.e., the set-apart-ness of God) which calls forth our worship, admiration, and praise. God's glory is the surpassing magnificence, beauty, and value of Who God is in all of His perfect characteristics: His perfect love, His sovereignty, His patience, His kindness, His wisdom, His loveliness, and all of His other perfections.

Grace the free, undeserved favor of God.

Holy set-apart, distinct, different, other; perfectly morally pure, sinless, upright, and containing nothing exceptionable.

Hope expectation, trust, confidence; properly, expectation of what is sure (certain); hope.

Human Spirit the breath or the life principle in living beings.

Humble lowly, in position or spirit (in a good sense) low; (figuratively) inner lowliness describing the person who depends on the Lord rather than self.

Humiliation is to make lower in rank, to make low or humble; to reduce to a lower position in one's own eyes or others' eyes.

Infallible not capable of making mistakes or being wrong.

Reconcile to bring back into a right relationship, or restore a broken relationship to a right relationship.

Regeneration the act or process of being born-again.

Repentance have a change of mind about our sin; to turn away from our sin, and towards God in the desire to live a God-glorifying life.

Righteous just; especially, just in the eyes of God; righteous; the elect (a Jewish idea).

Sanctification process of making or becoming holy, set apart, sanctification, holiness, consecration.

Sheol the grave, hell, or the pit.

Sin missing the mark; a fault, failure (in an ethical sense), a sinful deed.

Sovereign unrestricted in power and absolute domination, confessing no limitations or restraints.

Submission place under, subject to; mid, pass: I submit, put myself into subjection: "under God's arrangement," i.e. submitting to the Lord (His plan).

Trained (as used in Hebrews 12:11) (figuratively) to train with one's full effort, i.e. with complete physical, emotional force like when working out intensely in a gymnasium. In a figurative sense to train with one's full effort, i.e. with complete physical, emotional force as when working out intensely in a gymnasium; to exercise vigorously, in any way, either the body or the mind".

Questions? Comments? Testimonies?

**See www.boastinginweakness.com
Appropriating the Cross of Christ for Life.**